Alby and Me

John C Bird

Published by FeedARead.com Publishing – Arts Council funded.

A CIP catalogue record for this title is available from the British Library.

ALBY AND ME

Long-listed for the Waverton Good Read Award for Best Debut Novel.

'A fantastically touching tale. Everybody will find something in this book to relate to.' (Solihull Observer)

'Put simply, it is an enjoyable and emotionally gripping read, and one which left me wanting to go back and savour it again.' (Raw Edge)

It's a moving, humorous story of the friendship of two working class grammar school boys in their mid-teens... we are treated to what counts, to a story and an anguish that could apply in any decade.' (Author, journal of the Society of Civil and Public Service Writers)

'It's a rare yet delightful discovery... Alby and Me is marvellously written in strong concise prose, tells an excellent story and makes even the most ordinary issues fascinating.' (The Book Shelf blog)

'Alby and Me captured the post-war years in England with real insight. Just because the book features children it is not necessarily a children's book. Perhaps Alby and Me might be best suited to the historical fiction market, sitting alongside such titles as Angela's Ashes. (Harper Collins editor, Authonomy website)

A recommended holiday read. (Birmingham Life)

This novel is dedicated to the good folk of Birmingham, England, where I grew up. The story is set in a fictionalised version of the city as it was in the late 1940s. All the characters are imaginary, but I shouldn't be surprised if some of those with whom I shared my boyhood days think they recognise themselves.

For him in vain the envious seasons roll who bears eternal summer in his soul.
(Oliver Wendell Holmes 1809-1894)

CHAPTER ONE

Summer 1948

The creak of the loose floorboard on the landing woke me.
I knew it would be my father on his way downstairs. He
would be carrying his chamber pot, brimful and giving off
that familiar odour of the Ansells' mild ale he had imbibed
the night before at the Hare and Hounds. Bobbing about on
the surface would be a couple of butts from the Woodbines
he'd smoked before dropping off to sleep.

No need to look at my alarm clock. It would be
near enough a quarter past six. My father's routine hadn't
changed for as long as I could remember. Through the
open window I could hear the fluty melody of a blackbird,
which was soon interrupted by the insistent revving of
someone starting up a motorcycle. The early morning sun
filtered in through the yellow gingham curtains, bathing
my small bedroom in a soothing glow.

I began to feel pretty good about things, and then I
remembered what lay ahead at Herby's, aka Sir Herbert
Mason Grammar School, in just a few hours. The first
lesson of the morning was English Literature with Miss
Elspeth Dowdeswell MA (Cantab.), a woman of stentorian
voice and titanic bosom. 'Dowdy' struck fear into the heart
of all who sat before her, especially those of us who were
sometimes careless enough to drop our aitches or slur
words when reading aloud.

A lesson with Dowdy was daunting enough at any time but on this particular Monday morning it was an even more disquieting prospect. She would be announcing the results of the Fourth Form end-of-year English Literature examination, and woe betide anyone whose performance fell short of what she expected of them. Such unfortunate souls were likely to find themselves ordered to the front of the class and asked to explain why they had under-achieved. I had special reasons for not wanting to be among them on this occasion.

Close by in the foldaway bed, still sound asleep, was my best friend Alby Wilson, who always managed to do just as well as he wanted in examinations, and seemingly with minimal effort. He took care though, not to do too well and attract unwanted attention, either from the staff by seeming to be a bright, conscientious pupil with prefect potential, or from a group known as the Sharkey gang, who took a dim view of kids they considered to be swots.

Alby had the blankets pulled over his head, but I could hear his rhythmic breathing. He was stopping over at our house because his folks had been away for the weekend in their caravan. Alby thought the world of his mum and dad and his older sister, Enid, but didn't share their fondness for caravanning. Once when I asked him why, he looked at me as if I was a bit simple. 'How'd you like to be cooped up in a sweaty tin box with three other people all weekend? Wouldn't be so bad if you got a decent night's kip, but if it isn't my old man snoring, it's our Enid yakking in her sleep, or the cows mooing their udders off in the field next door.'

Downstairs I heard the hiss and hum of the

lavatory flushing, then the rattle of the plumbing as my father filled the kettle at the kitchen sink. The pipes went on juddering, and I knew he'd be washing his hands and face under the cold running water. Then everything went quiet. My father would be sitting at the kitchen table swigging a mug of strong, sweet tea. As always when he drank any hot liquid, each gulp would be followed by a throaty sigh as if he was sampling some rare vintage brandy. It was just one of his habits that set my teeth on edge.

My bedside clock showed twenty minutes to seven. Moments later I heard the front door slam, just as I knew it would. I sat up and lifted a corner of the curtain. My father was ambling up the gravel path that divided our small patch of front garden from that of the Powells next door. He was wearing a charcoal grey jacket and navy blue trousers salvaged from suits that had once been his Sunday best. Shiny patches on the elbows and on the seat of the trousers testified to years of service.

He stopped at the gate and lit a cigarette, then tossed the empty packet under the privet hedge before heading off along Jubilee Avenue to catch the bus to join the early shift at Burnsides' gas meter factory. As he disappeared in the distance, I noticed steam was beginning to rise from the road surface and the blue slate roofs of the houses. The sun crept slowly across the Thornfield estate over the houses and the chimneys and zigzag roofs of factories to the north. To the east I could see the tops of the cedar trees that stood like guardsmen around the edge of Chamberlain Park, the one reasonable-sized stretch of open space left in the neighbourhood.

Just visible on the far side of the park was the

silhouette of Sir Herbert Mason Grammar School, an ill-assorted mixture of gloomy Victorian architecture and modern appendages, which had replaced parts of the building demolished in a German bombing raid in 1942.

Apart from a couple of professional footballers and a soldier who won a VC in the First World War, Herby's couldn't boast many famous names among its pupils and was never a shining beacon of academic achievement. Most of the brightest kids went to the grammar schools in more affluent parts of the city. But I would have bet a year's pocket money there wasn't a sharper mind among the city's school population than the one presently slumbering a few feet away from me. In fact, such was his array of talents that I assumed someday he would be hailed as a genius in whatever field he decided to make his living. Then again, he was such a free spirit there were times when I felt that if it took his fancy he might just as easily choose to become a tramp or a beachcomber.

After watching my father go off to work, I dozed again until my mother came into the bedroom at about a quarter to eight. 'Your dinner money's on the sideboard, love,' she said. 'Make sure you and Alby have a hot drink and something to eat before you go to school. I'm off now.'

'Where are you working today?' I asked.

'The Farquhars,' she said. Her eyes looked tired and the taut ivory skin of her face   had a yellowish tinge.

Listening to her wheezy cough as she trudged downstairs, I thought of her having to kowtow to the snooty Mrs Farquhar, and felt a knot of frustration tighten in my chest. The Farquhars' house was among the largest on Northwood Avenue, which ran along one side of Chamberlain Park and was by some margin the most affluent road in the area. I realised my nails were digging into the palms of my hands as I clenched my fists under the sheets. Then I became aware that Alby had woken up and was lying watching me.

'You're looking a bit thoughtful, Matt old son,' he said.

'I'm feeling it,' I said.

'D'you want to tell your Uncle Albert all about it?'

'Not just at the moment.'

Alby pushed himself up on his elbows. 'In that case, how about a nice cup of tea?'

As I eased myself out of bed, Alby asked, 'What's the time?'

I picked up my clock and pointed the face towards him.

'Blimey, it's still only half way through the night,' he said, pulling his pillow over his head.

I went downstairs to the kitchen and put the kettle on. While I waited for the water to boil I cut four hunks off a cottage loaf, spread them with a thick layer of beef dripping, and put on some slices of beetroot. Then I made a pot of tea, poured two mugs, and carried them and the food on a tray up to the bedroom.

Alby breakfasted in bed. I ate and drank while I dressed, then headed downstairs again to wash at the kitchen sink. I knew from experience it wouldn't do much good nagging Alby to get a move on; he would go at his own pace come what may, so I sat at the kitchen table and read Sunday's *News of the World*.

With barely ten minutes left to catch the bus that would get us to school just in time to beat the assembly bell, Alby dashed into the kitchen, wet his comb under the tap and ran it quickly through his dark, curly hair. Then he splashed some cold water on his face and dabbed it dry on a hand towel before pulling on his green blazer and grabbing his satchel.

We sprinted down Jubilee Avenue to the corner of Stackley Road and leapt on a 44 bus just as it was about to pull out of the terminus.

'Cutting it fine aren't you, lads?' said the conductor as we scrambled, panting, onto the bench seat at the rear of the bus.

'Sorry about that,' said Alby, grinning. 'My mate here finds it hard getting up in the morning.'

As the bus headed off along the Stackley Road, Alby opened his satchel and pulled out a folded page from the Sporting Life and sat studying the runners at that day's race meeting at Folkestone.

'Don't forget it's English. Lit. first lesson,' I said,

'I haven't forgotten,' said Alby, without looking up.

'And Dowdy will be giving out the exam results.'

'I know. I'm not expecting any surprises. I should get between seventy and seventy-five percent.'

'How can you be so sure?'

'Because that's what I planned for. I know how Dowdy works out the marks.'

'Wish I could be so sure,' I said.

'Don't worry, you usually do okay.'

'I'd like to do a bit better than okay this time.'

'Why?'

'Dowdy's always going on at me for not coming up with the kind of work she reckons I'm capable of.'

Alby grinned. 'She's probably right. She usually

is.'

'I did some pretty serious revision for the exam,' I said. 'I'd like to do well enough to get Dowdy off my back. Also I reckon an "excellent" or a "very good" among the usual "satisfactorys" on my report would cheer up my mum. She's not been at all well lately.'

'You sure those are the only reasons for all the revising?' said Alby

'What other reason would I have?'

'Trying to impress a certain pretty girl maybe?'

I felt myself flush. Alby often teased me about my crush on our classmate Helen O'Donnell. Just thinking about her made the hairs on the back of my neck prickle. It wasn't just her looks and the lovely strawberry blonde hair, or the curves that even the regulation school gymslip couldn't conceal; it also had something to do with the serene purity she seemed to exude. Raymond Clegg, possessor of the Fourth Form's worst case of acne, probably got it just about right when he likened her to a combination of Ingrid Bergman and the Mona Lisa.

Alby grinned. 'You must be more smitten than I thought to put in all that extra homework.'

'That wasn't the main reason I did it,' I fibbed.

'Trouble is the beautiful Helen doesn't even know you fancy her,' said Alby.

'Would you like me to put in a good word for you?'

'No thanks.'

'Just trying to be helpful,' said Alby, holding up both hands. 'But she's never going to know how you feel about her if you don't say something. You need to get her on her own.' Alby stroked his chin. 'Let's see now, she usually walks home from school. If you happened to be hovering near the gates as she was leaving you could offer to walk her home.'

'Don't think I could do that.'

'Why not?'

'She's so… so confident, like all the kids from the big private houses. She'd probably tell me to get lost.'

' 'Don't be so sure. You're just as good as any of those posh kids, and a lot smarter than most of them.'

'It's okay for you,' I said, 'you're the most confident bugger in the school.'

'You have to believe in yourself before other folk will.'

It didn't help my confidence that Miss Dowdeswell seemed to pick on me more often than most others in the class, sometimes using me to demonstrate how the local accent could desecrate the Queen's English with an effectiveness possessed by few other dialects. Only the week before, after she had asked me to read a passage from Henry The Fourth Part One, she accused me of reducing the bard's glorious poetry to the level of a conversation in a fish and chip shop.

When I reminded Alby of Dowdy's remarks he laughed. 'Couldn't have put it better myself. Mind you, any of us from the estate could have murdered it just as well as you did.'

'Why do you reckon Dowdy picks on me?'

Alby assumed his wise adviser expression. 'Could be because you're shy.'

'Why should I get it in the neck for that?'

'The problem is it sometimes comes across as stubbornness. Can make you seem a bit bloody minded at

14

times. And there's another thing.'

'What's that?'

'Her tits.'

'What do you mean?'

'You know how when she's reading from her beloved Hardy or Dickens she gets all worked up and those huge knockers start bouncing around under her sweater like a couple of ferrets in a sack, you just sit and stare at them like you're hypnotised. She couldn't help but notice.'

'I bet you watch them as well.'

'Course I do, but I don't make it obvious like you. There could be another reason why Dowdy picks on you.'

'Oh yes,' I said, preparing myself for another of his shafts of wisdom.

'She fancies you, my son. Whenever an older woman lusts after a bloke much younger than herself, she takes it out on him to cover up her guilty feelings. Simple fact of life.'

'Don't talk daft,' I said, 'Dowdy must be knocking on fifty.'

'Interesting time of life for women,' Alby confided. 'Chemical changes happen in their bodies. They can't land up in the pudding club any more, and it makes them much more frisky.'

'Not Dowdy,' I said. 'I'm sure she wouldn't be the least bit interested in that kind of thing.'

Alby winked and shook his head. 'I wouldn't bet on it.'

Elspeth Dowdeswell's sex life was an ongoing source of speculation among the boys of the Fourth Form. Just the day before, during school dinner, it had been the main topic of conversation on our table. Opinion was fairly

15

evenly divided as to whether she was a nymphomaniac or a virgin, but there were dissenting voices. Dipper Dickson, the Fourth's generally acknowledged expert on sexual matters, suggested she might be a lesbian. Eddie Coates, who invariably occupied bottom place in English Literature examinations, wondered if she might be into bestiality, but those who had heard of the practice doubted its popularity with women. I was inclined to go along with the virginity theory. However hard I tried I found it impossible to imagine our regal English mistress in a writhing heap with a bloke doing the kind of things I'd read about in the dog-eared Hank Janson paperbacks that got passed around among the boys of the Fourth.

Dowdy's sexual proclivities, however, were the last thing on my mind as the bus pulled up at the stop opposite the great iron gates of Herbert Mason Grammar School. What seemed of paramount importance at that particular point in my life was the soon to be revealed results of the English Literature examination.

CHAPTER TWO

The Fourth Form was hushed as Miss Dowdeswell strode
into the classroom with a bulging manilla folder under her
arm. She was wearing a white polo neck sweater, but on
this occasion I managed to keep my eyes diverted from its
sumptuous contents. I looked across at Alby sitting at the
desk immediately to my left and he patted his chest with
both hands and winked.

Placing the folder on the desk, Dowdy adjusted her
horn-rimmed spectacles and looked slowly round the room.
'Dear me, I've seen happier faces at a funeral,' she said.
'Could it possibly be that some of you are awaiting the
results of the English Literature examination with less than
joyous anticipation?'

She opened the folder and took out a sheet and
perused it. 'Your marks in the   examination were generally
in line with what I would have expected, but with one
rather impressive exception.' Her gaze settled on me. 'The
top mark of eighty-six percent was achieved by Matthew
Sheridan, whose previous literary achievements have not,
shall we say, set the world alight. Stand up Sheridan and
tell the class how you raised your performance from
mediocre to excellent.'

My mouth had gone so dry, and all I managed to
croak was, 'I... I just did my best.'

'Hardly an enlightening analysis,' said Dowdy, 'but

I shall expect you to continue surprising me from here on.'

As I sat down, Helen O'Donnell, sitting near the front of the class, looked round and smiled, flashing perfect white teeth. The sun slanting in through the high windows created a halo around her head and made her hair shine like spun gold. My bliss was complete for maybe half a minute. Then Frankie Beckett, sitting immediately behind me, pushed a note into my hand. It carried a brief, chilling message: 'Arse licker. I'll see you at break.'

Frankie was the most feared pupil in the school, equally lethal with fists, head or his notorious steel-tipped boots. He was the kingpin in the Sharkey Gang, so called because most of its members lived on or near Sharkey Road, which ran through the more run-down part of the Thornfield estate. Many of the most troublesome families had been moved there when the city council began bulldozing the worst of the slums that ringed the inner city. The Sharkey Road houses were notorious for their neglected gardens, dirty, usually curtainless windows, and the drunken parties and fights that were a regular occurrence, especially at weekends.

The Sharkey Gang needed little excuse or encouragement to indulge their penchant for violence. Boys they saw as swots were among their favourite targets. I'd always managed to steer clear of trouble with the gang because I was careful never to display overt enthusiasm in the classroom by raising my hand in response to teachers' questions or engaging in class discussions, and until today had never shone in examinations. Also I managed to convey the impression that I shared the Sharkeys' devotion to the city football club, universally known to its supporters as *The Blues*. It helped too that I lived in one of the smaller houses on the Thornfield estate. Residents of the larger, so-called parlour-type houses, who paid a higher rent, were regarded by the Sharkeys as being at best snobs and at worst traitors to the working class.

I was barely paying attention as Dowdy read out the rest of the examination results and proceeded to go over the questions and the kind of answers most likely to impress markers for the School Certificate examinations we would be sitting the following year. As I watched the classroom clock it seemed to move with alarming speed towards 10.20, when the bell would ring for morning break, I cursed myself for revising so hard for the English Literature examination. I couldn't imagine Alby getting so carried away; not that he ever needed to do much revision. Once he had heard or read anything, no matter how boring or abstruse, he seemed able to file it away in his mind for instant recall whenever he needed it.

I passed Frankie's note across the aisle to Alby. Soon after he returned it with the scribbled words 'Don't worry, we'll figure something out.' Knowing Alby's resourcefulness, his words gave me a little comfort, but I continued to wrack my brain for some kind of excuse to offer Frankie. Maybe I could say I'd worked hard for the examination to win a bet. No, I couldn't see him swallowing that. What if I said I'd copied Pauline Wagstaffe, who sat at the next desk to mine in the examination, and was acknowledged to be red hot at English Literature? But how would I explain getting a better mark than her? It was no use, I knew that even a doctor's certificate confirming an incurable brain disease and giving me only three months to live would leave Frankie unmoved. His heart was as hard as the metal toecaps of his boots.

When the bell rang and the classroom emptied, I stayed put and Alby remained behind with me. We sat in silence for a few moments, then Alby said, 'Knowing Frankie, there's one thing that might save your bacon.'

'What's that?'

'Bribery,' he said.

'I haven't got anything to bribe him with.'

'You sure? Doesn't have to be cash. Maybe you could offer him that new table tennis bat you got for your birthday, or nick him a packet of your dad's ciggies.'

Before I could respond, Frankie appeared in the classroom doorway with Lenny Bradd and Mick Golding, two other Sharkey gang members 'You two coming out to play?' said Frankie, with his trademark sneer.

'Wonder Sheridan hasn't got his nose buried in the cushion on Dowdy's chair,' said Lenny, moving towards me. Frankie nudged him aside and stepped forward.

'So,' he said, his face almost touching mine, 'we've decided to become teacher's little crawler have we?'

'No, Frankie,' I said, trying to keep the fear out of my voice, 'it was one of those freak results; you know, like a Third Division team beating the Blues. I just wrote down the first stuff that came into my head, and got lucky.'

Frankie stared at me. 'I'd say you got unlucky. And I'd say you're a lying git. You swotted your bollocks off, didn't you?'

'Come on, Frankie,' Alby intervened. 'Matt's no crawler. Dowdy had probably been knocking back the hard stuff when she marked his paper.'

Frankie ignored him and turned to his pals. 'What'll

20

we do with teacher's little darling?'

Before Lenny and Mick could offer suggestions, I had one of those flashes of inspiration that sometimes seem to arrive out of nowhere when all seems lost. 'Fancy going to the Blues' game on Saturday, Frankie?' I heard myself saying with a calmness I could hardly credit. 'Got a couple of tickets for the best seats in the ground; in the centre stand where the VIPs sit. Would you like them?' The club were newly promoted to the First Division of the Football League, and I knew Frankie would kill for the best tickets to their first home match of the season.

'You'd better not be bullshitting,' he said. 'How'd you get hold of those kind of tickets?'

I explained that Sam Elliman, a Blues director, was one of my mum's house cleaning clients, and he'd given her the tickets for my father to use. It wasn't the first time Mr Elliman had sent my father complimentary tickets which, unknown to the donor, he invariably sold on to cronies more addicted to football than himself.

'Make sure you bring the tickets to school in the morning,' said Frankie, fixing me with his pale blue eyes. 'Or else…'

After the Sharkeys had gone, Alby stuck up a thumb. 'Told you bribery would do the trick.'

'I think I just signed my death warrant,' I said. 'My old man will murder me when he finds the Cup tickets have disappeared. He'll know straight away who took them.'

'How?'

'Well, my mum's hardly likely to nick them is she? And there's no-one else in the house. Anyway I wouldn't be able to lie to him. He'd know in a flash.'

'Yes, I can see it's going to be a bit tricky.'

21

'Maybe I should throw myself off the school roof now.'

Alby grinned. 'Nah, that'd be messy. Your best plan might be to disappear for a couple of days, then when you turn up again your folks would be so happy to see you they'd forgive anything.'

'You're full of bright ideas,' I said.

'Don't worry,' said Alby, 'it'll work out. Meanwhile I've got something to cheer you up.'

'Not one of your jokes.'

'No, this is deadly serious. A couple of stonewall certainties running at Kempton Park.'

'Think I've lived dangerously enough for one day,' I said. 'Anyway I can't afford to bet on horses.'

'But you can't lose on this one,' Alby insisted. 'These gee-gees were tipped by Captain Winsome.'

'Who's he?'

'A professional tipster. Best in the business. Hangs out at Newmarket; knows all the trainers and jockeys. My dad and his mates chip in two bob each for his tips every week.'

'I told you, I'm skint.'

'You've got your school dinner money.'

I hesitated, then I remembered the school dinner menu on Mondays was usually toad in the hole with jam tart and custard for afters. It was sufficient to kill off what little appetite I had left after my run-in with Frankie. 'All right, count me in for a bob then,' I said. 'Anything for a quiet life.'

Alby pulled a folded page from *Sporting Life* from his blazer pocket and opened it up. After studying it for a couple of minutes, he said, 'We'll have a two-bob double.

If both nags come up at these prices, we'll win nearly two quid apiece.'

'What are their names?' I asked, deciding I'd better show at least a passing interest in my investment.

'Diamond King and Cabin Boy,' said Alby heading for the door. 'Have to dash now, I'm busting for a pee.'

At lunch-time we slipped out of school across the playing field and squeezed through a narrow gap in a hedge beyond which was the car park of the Green Lion pub. Alby led the way to a side door and pushed it open. 'Come on,' he said, 'there's nobody about.'

The mingling odours of stale tobacco smoke and disinfectant greeted us as we hurried along the corridor to where the gents' toilet was situated. Alby opened the door and peered in, then slipped inside, beckoning me to follow. The end one of a row of four cubicles had an *Out of Order* notice pinned to the door. Alby gave the door three quick raps and called out, 'All right, Percy?'

'Who's that?' a gruff voice demanded.

'Alby. Alby Wilson.'

The door was opened by a gaunt-faced old man in a pullover and stained pair of khaki army surplus trousers. 'Allo young Alby,' said the bookie's runner, his smile revealing a row of yellow tombstones. 'Who's your mucker, then?'

'Matt Sheridan, my best mate.'

'Orl right, s'long as his old man ain't a rozzer.'

Alby grinned. 'No, he's okay; straight as a dog's hind leg.'

'Let's be 'aving yer bet then,' said Percy.

Alby pushed a scrap of paper wrapped around two

shilling coins into the grubby, tobacco-stained hand. 'I'll pick up the winnings about the same time tomorrow,' he said, with a wink.

'Expect you will,' Percy cackled, 'knowing what a lucky young sod you are.'

As we re-emerged into the corridor, Alby said, 'Come on, it's all quiet, let's go out the front way and back along the Stackley Road. I'm feeling a bit peckish.'

When we reached the shopping parade, we stopped outside the Co-op grocery and gazed through the big curved windows at the open tins of Huntley and Palmers assorted biscuits and trays of cooked meats. As we inhaled the savoury, spicy aromas drifting through the open door, Alby said, 'I'm bloody starving.'

'Me too,' I said.

'Haven't got any cash left have you?' Alby asked.

'Not a bean,' I said. 'All I had was my dinner money, and that's gone on the horses.'

As we came up to Pecks' greengrocery shop Alby paused and glanced around. Then, quick as lightning, he grabbed two Conference pears from a display rack in front of the shop and slipped one in each of his trouser pockets. We hurried on and when we were well clear of the shopping parade, he handed me one of the pears and started munching the other. 'That was a blow for the working class,' he said.

'What, nicking Pecks' fruit?' I said.

'Sid Peck's a Tory councillor, isn't he?' said Alby. 'His party looks after the toffs. I'd never nick anything from an outfit like the Co-op; that's run for the benefit of ordinary working folk.'

'You reckon its okay to pinch from people just

24

because they're Tories?'

'There's an even better reason in Sid's case,' said Alby. 'He's doing the dirty on his missus; having it off with Lucy Simmons.'

Lucy worked at Spicers' Newsagents next door but one to the Pecks' shop. She had a reputation, deserved or not, of dispensing her sexual favours rather freely, and lately rumours had been circulating that she and Sid Peck were having an affair.

'It's only rumours,' I said.

'Nah, it's more than that,' said Alby. 'Dipper Dickson saw them walking hand in hand in Stratford a couple of weeks ago.'

'Maybe they're just friends.'

'And maybe I'm the Duke of Windsor,' said Alby. 'Anyway, don't go all righteous on me; you've been known to wangle a few bob out of the Tories yourself before now. Remember the last election?'

Alby and me had worked for the Conservatives collecting registration cards and asking people how they voted as they came out of the polling station at Palmerston Lane School. We had offered our services to the Conservatives after we discovered that they paid four shillings for the day compared to the half a crown offered by the Labour Party.

Alby began to sing:

> *Vote vote vote for Harry Horsfall,*
> *who's that knocking on my door?*
> *If it's Welsby or his wife,*
> *we will stab 'em with a knife,*
> *and they won't come knocking any more.*

It was a refrain the kids on our estate used to

launch into whenever they caught sight of the Labour candidate, Harry Horsfall, or his Conservative opponent, Nigel Welsby, out campaigning.

'Remember how we chucked away half the cards we'd collected to bugger up the Tories' sums?' Alby chuckled.

'My old man approved of that,' I said. 'It was the only thing that stopped him thumping me when he found out I'd worked for the Conservatives.'

Alby bit into his pear. 'You haven't got a lot of time for your old man, have you?'

'You could say that.'

'It's a lottery really,' said Alby.

'What is?'

'The kind of parents you land up with. Just hard cheese if they're evil buggers, or always skint, or thick as two planks. They could just as easily have been stinking rich clever sods with hearts of gold.'

Alby finished his last mouthful of pear and tossed the core over a privet hedge into somebody's front garden. 'With a bit of luck the seeds'll take and those people will end up with a nice pear tree… Shame our dads don't get on. They used to be such good mates, just like us.'

'It's my old man's fault,' I said.

'I dunno,' said Alby, 'There's probably a bit of blame on both sides. My dad practically accused yours of being a coward in the war. No wonder he took offence.'

'I think they'd both had a bit too much to drink the night they fell out.' I said.

'Daft really,' said Alby, 'how they've ended up feuding like the bloody mafia. Wish we could figure out some way to get 'em speaking to each other again.'

'Easier said than done.'

'There's got to be a way,' said Alby.

I said I had my doubts when somebody was as stubborn as my father.

Alby scratched his chin. 'Let's think about it.'

'Know what,' I said, 'I've always envied you your dad.' I wished I had a father I could like, let alone love like you're supposed to.'

'Did you ever stop and think what might have made your old man the way he is?'

'Not really.'

'Maybe he was knocked about as a kid; perhaps his dad was a devil worshipper, or his mum forced him to eat swedes or sago pudding. Things like that can do terrible things to young minds.'

I was never quite sure when Alby was being serious.

As we entered the school playground a noisy game of football was in progress. Thirty or more lads were chasing an old tennis ball around like a swarm of locusts. We joined in, but had barely had time to raise a sweat when the bell sounded for the afternoon session. Ahead lay double lessons of Woodwork and Scripture.

'Never mind,' said Alby as we drifted into the Woodwork room. 'There's always some bugger worse off than yourself. Think about poor old Jesus. When he was our age he got nothing but carpentry and religion all day long.'

But my mind was on less pious matters, like the Sharkeys, football tickets and my father's unpredictable temper. My brain stubbornly refused to concentrate on scholastic matters. As we trudged out of the classroom after

27

the final lesson, Alby put his arm around my shoulder. 'I know we've just suffered an hour and a half of Scripture,' he said, 'but you look really like you're expecting the end of the world before teatime.'

'That's about how I feel,' I said.

'You could try walking across the playground beating your chest and wailing 'Woe is me for I am undone.'

'Isaiah chapter six, verse five,' I said.

Alby nodded. 'If we hadn't just been studying Izzy's bit in the Old Testament I'd have given you ten out of ten for remembering that.'

'Blow Isaiah,' I said, 'I wish you could come up with something helpful.'

Alby's face brightened. 'I think I can. I've just had a vision. Right there ahead of us.

'What vision?'

'Helen O'Donnell. She's just heading out of the school gate.'

'Yes, I see her, but what…' I began.

'No buts,' said Alby. 'Go on after her. She's on her own. Ask if she'd mind you walking along with her.'

'I couldn't do that.'

'Of course you can. She'll be fascinated to talk to the guy who's just come top of the form in her favourite subject.'

'Do you really think so?'

'Trust me.' Alby gave me a gentle push forward. 'Go on or you'll be too late.'

'Okay, but I'll strangle you if this goes wrong,' I said, quickening my step until I caught up with Helen a few yards beyond the gate.

'Hi.' I said, 'mind if I walk along with you?'

'I thought you usually went home on the bus,' she said.

'I do,' I said, 'but I fancied a walk today.'

'But isn't it out of your way going in this direction.'

It was, I said, but not much. And any way it was nice to go a different way home sometimes.

'Okay if you want to,' she said. 'Well done in the exam, by the way.'

'Probably a flash in the pan,' I said.

She smiled. 'Don't be so modest.'

I felt myself flush. 'I did do more revision than usual.'

'Do you enjoy English Lit?'

'Yes, it's one of my favourite subjects.'

'Mine too.'

'I find Miss Dowdeswell a bit formidable though,' I said, feeling pleased I had come up with a word like *formidable* at a moment when I was feeling so nervous.

Helen nodded. 'I suppose she can be, but she's a brilliant teacher.'

I agreed, and tried to think of some gambit to switch the conversation from scholastic matters to more interesting topics like what Helen did in the evenings and at weekends and had she seen the film currently showing at the local Odeon.

'Got quite a bit of home work tonight,' I said feebly.

Helen patted her satchel. 'Yes, so have I, but never mind, it's nearly end of term. Will you be going anywhere interesting on holiday?'

'Probably to my aunt's in Shrewsbury.'

'That should be nice.'

'How about you?'

'We're going to the Isle of Wight. Daddy's keen on sailing and has a boat down there.'

I couldn't think of an appropriate response. I tried to come up with something witty to change the subject, but my mind went blank. After we had walked in silence for a short while Helen looked at me, smiling. 'You're quite shy aren't you?'

I felt an embarrassing flush creeping up my neck. 'Do you think so?'

'Yes I do.'

'I'm sorry, I…'

'Oh don't worry about it, I think it's rather sweet. You are the complete opposite of your friend, Alby Wilson. He always seems so confident, so worldly wise.'

'I suppose he does.'

'He'll go a long way.'

'I'm certain he will.'

I began to feel frustrated that our conversation had not got beyond the superficial and seemed to have got around to comparing me rather unfavourably with Alby, however justified that comparison might be.

As we neared the gates of Chamberlain Park, Helen suggested that we took the path that cut across a corner of the park that came out near her house. A group of young children and a two dogs were involved in a noisy game of tag along one side of the path, watched by two beaming elderly women seated on a bench enjoying the late afternoon sunshine. They smiled at us as we passed and I felt a surge of pride to be seen with Helen at my side.

30

'It wasn't an accident that I happened to meet you at the school gate,' I heard myself saying. 'I just wanted an excuse to walk home with you.'

Helen laughed. 'I did wonder,' she said.

'I hope you didn't mind.'

'I'm quite flattered.'

As we reached the gate of her house, Helen turned and smiled, 'It was sweet of you to walk home with me,' she said, then hurried up the drive. As she opened the large studded oak door she waved before disappearing into the house.

I felt like singing as I made my way back across the park. The old ladies were still sitting on the bench and they gave me a friendly wave as I went past. A couple of hours earlier I would not have dared to imagine that I, the shy, awkward Matt Sheridan, would escort home the most beautiful, desirable girl at Herby's. Now I was already having visions of her nestling up to me in the back row of the Odeon and reclining in the stern seat of a rowing boat as I propelled it round the lake in Chamberlain Park. But then I decided I was reading far too much into something to which the lovely Helen would probably not even give a second thought. Whatever happened though, in the past few minutes the world had became a more joyful place. I believed I had fallen in love.

My first thought was to go straight round to Alby's house and tell him about it, but then I decided that such moments were too precious to share even with your best friend. And in any case I would not have wanted Helen to think I was going around boasting. Knowing how gossip spread around Herby's and the Thornfield estate, such a titbit could easily end up with people saying I had claimed

31

to have had it off with Helen. I resolved not to say a word to anyone.

The euphoria of my brief time alone with Helen soon began to dissipate though, as I walked on. By the time I reached the Thornfield estate my father and the football tickets had ousted Helen from my thoughts.

When I got home my mother was in the kitchen preparing the evening meal.

'You're late,' she said. 'I was beginning to get a little worried.'

'I got chatting to someone and came a different way home,' I said.

'Must have been someone interesting to go out of your way.'

'She was, very interesting.'

'Oh a *she,* eh?'

'Just someone from my form.'

'And where does she live?'

'Up by Chamberlain Park. Northwood Avenue.'

'In one of the big private houses?'

'Yes.'

'Hope it's not one where I go cleaning.'

'I don't think so.'

'What's the family's name?'

'O'Donnell.'

'No, it's not one of my houses, thank goodness.'

'Would it matter?'

'I don't expect any of the people up there would want their charlady's son walking their daughter home. Not that you're not just as good as any of the people who live in those private houses.'

'I'm sure the O'Donnells aren't snobs,' I said, 'not with a daughter as nice as Helen.'

My mother placed saucepans of potatoes and cauliflower on the gas stove and lit the jets under them. 'I get the impression you're keen on the young lady,' she said.

'Don't jump to conclusions, mum,' I said. 'All I've done is walk home once with her.'

My mother laughed. 'We shall see.'

'Don't hold your breath,' I said. 'Anyway, what's for dinner?'

'Pork chops with apple sauce and stuffing.'

'My favourite,' I said, though my appetite had suddenly deserted me. I could see the football tickets in the place my father had left them behind the coronation mug on the shelf above the gas stove. After my mother had gone into the living room to listen to the early evening news on the wireless, I reached up and, with a trembling hand, took the tickets and put them in my pocket.

CHAPTER THREE

The assembly hall at Herby's was a dark, cavernous place enclosed on all sides by classrooms. Oak panelled walls stretched from the floor to the balcony which circled the hall and gave access to the upper floor classrooms. The little clusters of hanging lights in the high ceiling were inadequate for the size of the hall and merely added to its gloomy ambience.

On this Tuesday morning as I shuffled into the hall for school assembly I spotted Alby sitting half-way along one side in the shadow cast by the balcony. As I sat down beside him on the wooden block floor, he said, 'You look like you've lost a quid and found a tanner. Don't tell me you couldn't get those tickets for Frankie?'

'I've got them alright,' I said. 'I'm just thinking about what my old man will do when he finds they're gone.'

'You could just plead ignorance,' said Alby. 'Your dad couldn't prove you've nicked them. They might have been swiped by a burglar, or eaten by mice or...'

'Come on Alby,' I said, 'it's nothing to joke about.'

Alby stroked his chin thoughtfully. 'Maybe you could get your mum to have a word with him, appeal to his paternal instincts; tell him the tickets were the only thing that saved his son getting done over by the Sharkey Gang.'

'Don't think he has such things as paternal instincts.'

'He must have some. Even wild animals have them; that's what makes them protect their young from predators that'd like to have them for dinner.'

'Anyway I wouldn't want to get my mum involved,' I said. 'She has a bad enough time with the old man as it is.'

'I think we're running a bit short of options, mate,' said Alby. 'Only one thing left.'

'What's that?'

'The Big Fellah. Have a word with him.'

'Don't you think he'd take a dim view of me pinching the tickets?'

'In the circs I reckon he might be pretty sympathetic.'

Before I could respond the chattering hubbub around us suddenly went quiet. At the front of the hall the black-gowned figure of the Headmaster, Dr Lang (aka the Beak), was stepping up onto the stage to begin the assembly. The opening hymn, he announced, was *Praise My Soul The King of Heaven,* which happened to be one of my favourites. Unfortunately someone nearby coughed as the Beak announced the page number in our hymn books and we didn't hear it. Miss Wilkes, the music teacher, launched into the familiar opening bars on the piano and most of the assembled pupils were singing the alleluias near the end of the first verse by the time Alby and me found the correct page in the hymn book. We both gave an extra lusty rendering of the last line *'Praise with us the god of grace'* to make up for what we had missed.

As the school ploughed on with the hymn, I whispered to Alby, 'Do you really think the Big Fellah might help me out over the tickets?'

35

'I've got every confidence in him,' said Alby.

'What do you reckon he might do?'

Alby put a hand on my shoulder. 'Hard to say, mate. He can be a bit unpredictable. Folk who know about these things say he moves in mysterious ways, but I've got a feeling in my water he'll see you okay in the end.'

Alby had a knack of sounding reassuring even when his actual words were not particularly so, and I began to feel a little less despondent. In fact I think the Big Fellah would have been quite pleased with the enthusiasm I was able to put into the last verse of the hymn, even though the words Alby and me sang were not the ones in the hymnal, but a version we had dreamed up ourselves:

Angels in big hats exploring,
Blow a raspberry in your face;
Saints triumphant, started snoring,
Gabby Thacker wears a brace.
Alleluia! Allellulia!
Praise with us old W G Grace.

Alby and me had different versions for many of the hymns regularly used in school assemblies and I often felt a little guilty singing them. Alby, though, had no qualms. He was sure the Big Fellah had a sense of humour and that in any case he probably got tired of hearing the same old words all the time. I just hoped none of the teachers seated along each side of the hall heard the words we sang as I doubted they would share the Big Fellah's sense of humour.

I tried hard to concentrate during the Beak's prayer which followed the hymn, and after that as we said the Lord's Prayer. My mind, though, began wandering during the bible reading by the head prefect, A. F. J. Oxley, and I

36

heard little of the final blessing by Dr Lang or his announcements which followed. By this time I'd spotted Frankie Beckett and Mick Golding watching me from a few rows back.

As I headed towards the stairs with Alby to go up the classroom for our first lesson of the day, which happened to be German, Frankie and Mick were waiting for me in the stairwell. They said nothing; Frankie simply held out his hand. I reached in my satchel, pulled out the football tickets, and placed them in the proffered hand. Frankie examined them briefly, nodded and strode off followed by Mick.

'What a couple of charmers,' said Alby as we climbed the stairs.

'I'm not bothered,' I said, 'as long as I've got Frankie off my back.'

During the next half hour Fraulein Irma Kueng, a petite blonde exchange teacher from Austria, briefly diverted my mind from such matters as football tickets and fathers and retribution. But my concentration began to waver as we grappled with the complexities of irregular verbs and present indicatives.The only lively interlude was when Eddie Coates asked our heavily accented instructor if she had been a member of the Hitler Youth organisation.

'I shall ignore that question,' said Fraulein Kueng, 'it's not worthy of an answer.'

'It's quite okay if you have,' said Alby, 'we know it was only like belonging to the Boy Scouts or Girl Guides here.'

Fraulein Kueng flushed. 'Can we please get on with the lesson.'

'Ja wohl,' someone behind me whispered in the

clipped speech of a stage German. 'Ve must obey orders at all times.' The teacher could hardly have missed the muffled sniggers and I felt sorry for her. I think Alby must have felt sympathy too, because when she asked for a volunteer to read out a passage from the text book about the historic city of Bonn, he was the first to raise his hand. He read it faultlessly and was warmly praised by the teacher.

'Never known you to volunteer like that before,' I said as we ambled out of the classroom en-route for our next lesson.

'Felt really sorry for the Fraulein,' said Alby. 'Anyway it was a bit of fun getting my throat round some of those German words. Mind you, I wouldn't have volunteered if Frankie or his mates had been in the class.'

'I'm fed up of worrying about Frankie,' I said. 'How did our horses get on yesterday?'.

'They ran well,' said Alby.

'How much did we win?' I asked.

'Well, nothing actually.'

'I thought you said our horses ran well.'

'They did. Diamond King won by three lengths and Cabin boy was leading 'til he was brought down by another nag a furlong from home. Terrible luck, but we bet on a double so both our horses needed to win. Never mind, we'll clean up next time.'

I wished I shared Alby's optimism, not just about picking winners but about life in general. What little optimism I still possessed was dwindling rapidly as the school day wore on and the time to go home approached.

CHAPTER FOUR

I was sitting at the living room table doing my History homework when my father came home from work. He greeted me with a nod and a gruff 'All right?' As he crossed the room to hang his jacket in the usual place on the back of the stairs door I caught a whiff of the familiar oily metallic smell of the factory.

He turned and shuffled back across the room and sank into the green moquette armchair in front of the fire. Bending forward, he took off his boots and socks, wrapped one of the socks around an oil-ingrained finger, and began painstakingly wiping away the sweaty accretion between each of his toes. It was a ritual I witnessed most weekday evenings and the gorgonzola smell of his foot sweat never failed to make me feel a little nauseous. When he'd finished he reached for the battered Fry's cocoa tin in the hearth, withdrew a Woodbine stub and placed it between his lips. He tore a thin strip from the back page of the *Evening Mail*, rolled it into a spill, and poked it through the bars of the coal fire. The spill flared and he lifted it quickly and lit his cigarette before tossing the blackened paper onto the fire.

Drawing deeply on the cigarette, my father sighed and sank deeper into his chair, stretching his bare feet across the rug. He sat staring at the dancing flames reflected in the polished black grate until the cigarette burned too short to hold, then flicked the stub into the fire. Soon his eyes closed and heavy breathing gradually gave way to rhythmic snoring in sync with the rise and fall of a belly nurtured in the saloon bar of the Hare and Hounds. The top buttons of his collarless shirt were undone, exposing pale, hairless flesh and the faded blue tattoo of the dragon on his chest. Above his collar line the white skin changed abruptly to crimson, which turned darker around his nose and cheeks.

He was still sleeping when my mother came home. She had been working late at one of the big houses near Chamberlain Park and on her way home had called at the Jubilee fish bar to collect three helpings of cod and chips for our dinner. The aroma of the fried food made me salivate as she unwrapped the layers of newspaper and put the meal in the oven to warm while she laid the table and made a pot of tea. When everything was ready she woke my father and gave him his dinner on a tray while she and I ate at the table.

After he'd cleared his plate and smoked another cigarette, my father went upstairs to change out of his working clothes. Soon I heard the clump clump of darts hitting the board hung on the back of the kitchen door. He always practised before going to play for the Hare and Hounds' team on Wednesday evenings in the Thornfield and District Darts League. After a few minutes the sound of the darts ceased and my father appeared in the kitchen doorway. 'Anybody seen those Blues tickets?'

'They were behind the coronation mug on the kitchen shelf,' said my mother.

'I know that,' said my father, his voice rising. 'They're not there now. What's happened to them?'

I felt panic clawing at my throat.

'Well, come on,' said my father. 'Somebody's

shifted them.'

'I took them,' I heard myself blurt out.

'What you done with them?'

'I gave them away.'

My father strode across the room to where I was sitting. 'You did what?'

'I gave them to Frankie Beckett. He and his mates were going to beat me up.'

My father stared at me. 'I've got a customer at the pub waiting to pay me the full whack for those tickets.' One of his large hands clamped onto the back of my neck and steered me towards the front door. 'Get yourself round to the Becketts' now,' he said, 'and don't come back without them tickets.'

My mother stood up, her pale face pinched with alarm. 'Please George, don't make Matt do that. You know what the Becketts are like. They're an awful family. Goodness knows what they'll do.'

The veins in my father's cheeks turned a deeper shade of purple. 'Stay out of this woman. I want those tickets back.'

'Frankie won't give them back,' I pleaded, 'I know he won't.'

'Then you'll bloody well have to make him,' said my father, opening the door.

My mother grabbed my jacket, which had been draped over the back of a chair and handed it to me. 'Do be careful, love,' she whispered.

As the door closed behind me I could hear my father's voice drowning out that of my mother. Once outside I felt a mixture of relief and dread; relief to be out of my father's presence and dread at what lay ahead.

41

It had been raining and the air smelt fresh and cool. As I trudged along the wet, deserted road past the familiar houses, I glimpsed people I knew inside and envied them their cosy havens of safety. At the corner of Sharkey Road I stopped under a street lamp, finding momentary comfort in the oasis of light. Then I turned and walked quickly until I reached the gate of the Becketts' house. I couldn't see any lights inside.   Maybe there was no-one at home. My hopes rose. Perhaps I wouldn't have to face Frankie after all. I hesitated, took several deep breaths, then walked up the path and gave the door knocker a firm rap. After a few moments there were sounds from the back of the house. A light came on and the door was opened by Mrs Beckett, a stout peroxide blonde with a carelessly powdered face. She eyed me suspiciously. 'Yeh, what is it?'

'Is Frankie in?'

'Who wants him?'

I resisted an urge to run and managed to croak my name.

Mrs Beckett turned and yelled, 'Frankie, somebody at the door for you.'

Frankie appeared wearing a vest and a pair of tight black trousers. He looked puzzled to see me. 'What you want?'

I swallowed hard. 'It's about the tickets for the Blues' match…' I began.

'What about 'em?'

'My old man wants them back.'

'You what?' A sneer spread over his face.

'No I mean it. My father…'

'Piss off, and tell your old man to do the same.'

'But Frankie, I…'

42

Before I could finish Frankie had slammed the door. I stood staring, unfocussed, for several moments, then shuffled off down the path. I felt limp and miserable as I trudged back along Sharkey Road. When I reached the turning for Jubilee Avenue I stopped once more under the street lamp. It had begun drizzling again and I stared absently at the light above, hoping for some inspiration as to what to do next. As I watched the rivulets of rainwater running down the lamp glass and plopping onto the pavement below like teardrops, my mind was churning over the sequence of events that had led to my present predicament. At that moment I wasn't sure who I despised most - my father, Frankie or myself, but one thing I was sure of was that bullies and cowards were equally contemptible. I also knew I had no control over what my father and Frankie did; I was only responsible for my own actions.

A motor bike roared past and the noise seemed to jerk my brain out of its paralysis. Suddenly, as if impelled by some invisible force, I found myself striding back towards the Becketts' house. By the time I reached the garden gate my heart was beating a drumroll on my ribcage. Almost immediately I heard the front door open and slam and the sound of heavy boots on the concrete path. Frankie saw me as he opened the gate and stepped out onto the pavement. 'What the fuck are you doing here? I thought I'd told you to get lost.'

'I've got to have those tickets back,' I said.

He put his hand into the pocket of his bomber jacket, took out the tickets and waved them in front of my face. 'D'ya mean these? Carry 'em with me all the time.'

'Why do you do that?'

43

'Make sure my old man or nobody else nicks 'em.'

'I can't go home without them, Frankie,' I said.

'Well you'll have to kip on the street then, won't you.' Frankie pushed me aside and started to walk on.

I grabbed his arm. 'Frankie, I've got to…'

'You're really beginning to get on my wick now,' he said. 'Why don't you bugger off before you get hurt.'

As he turned to walk away I snatched the tickets from his hand, but he reacted with lightning reflexes, grabbing my shirt and jerking me forward. I smelled the whiff of Brylcreem as his head rammed into my face, then felt the blood oozing from my nose and down over my mouth and chin. As I tried to step back his knee thudded into my groin and I fell gasping onto the pavement. Through a haze of pain I saw Frankie drawing his boot back to deliver another kick. Somehow I managed to throw myself forward and smother it, causing Frankie to stumble and fall on top of me. As we rolled, wrestling into the gutter, I used all the strength I had left to push hard against his muscular neck. He pitched sideways and there was a dull thud as his head hit the kerb. He lay still for several moments, then tried to lever himself up into a sitting position. The effort proved too much and he slumped back, gasping, his shoulders on the pavement and legs stuck out into the gutter, which was still running with muddy rainwater.

I lay beside him, aching and breathless, wondering how badly hurt he was. I had heard of people getting a bang on the head and dying of brain damage and haemorrhages. I found myself mouthing a silent prayer: 'Please God don't let Frankie die.'

With a struggle that made the sweat run down my

forehead into my eyes, I managed to get shakily to my feet, hooked my hands under Frankie's armpits, and pulled him almost upright. Supporting him from behind, I dragged him like a floppy doll up the path to his front door, and banged on the knocker.

Mrs Beckett came to the door. She gasped when she saw her son standing there swaying, eyes glazed, blood dribbling from his mouth. 'What you done to him?' she screeched.

'It was an accident,' I said. 'We got into a scrap and he fell and cracked his head on the kerb.'

Pulling Frankie inside, she managed to manoeuvre him into a chair near the door, where he slumped back silent and expressionless. His mother glared at me. 'Good job for you his dad's not here.'

'Hope he's going to be okay,' I said.

'He'd better be, or Christ help you. What you come round here for anyway. Looking for trouble were you?'

'No, I just wanted to talk to Frankie.'

'What were you fighting about then?'

'These,' I said, holding up the tickets.

'What are they?'

'Tickets for a football match.'

'You ain't heard the last of this,' she shouted as I walked off down the path as smartly as my aching limbs would allow. I had no doubt she was right.

When I got home Alby had just arrived. I'd forgotten we had arranged to go round to Dipper Dickson's house to play Monopoly.

'Blimey,' Alby greeted me, 'you look like you've been through a meat grinder.'

'Have a bit of trouble with young Beckett, did you?'

said my father.

'A bit,' I said, tossing the tickets on the table.

My father picked them up and examined them like they were laboratory specimens. 'You'd better clean yourself up before your mother sees you,' he said.

I went into the kitchen followed by Alby and looked in the mirror over the sink. A grazed bruise covered most of my left cheek and my right eye was blackened and almost closed. My hair was matted with blood and dirt and the front of my shirt looked like I'd been pelted with overripe tomatoes.

I soaked a flannel under the tap and wiped the blood and mess from my face and hair, then went upstairs to change my clothes. Alby followed, quizzing me about the fight.

When I told him how Frankie had hit his head on the kerb and how I had deposited him at his front door in a semi-conscious state, Alby shook his head slowly. 'You realise what this means, don't you?'

'Yes,' I said. 'It means Frankie will murder me as soon as he gets over his headache. Always assuming he does get over it.'

'How bad was he when you left him?' said Alby.

'Seemed really groggy. I just hope he hasn't got brain damage.'

' Frankie's a hard case,' said Alby, 'I'm sure he'll be okay. And you'll be a folk hero. The kid who laid Frankie Beckett out cold.'

'Come off it, Alby,' I said. 'Frankie would have slaughtered me if he hadn't accidentally caught his head on the kerb.'

Alby smiled. 'A minor detail, old son.'

When we went back downstairs my mother had just returned. 'My God, what's happened to you?' Her voice was shaking. 'Look at your face.'

'I fell over on the road,' I said. 'Just got a bump and a couple of bruises.'

My mother shook her head. 'It was that Frankie Beckett, wasn't it?'

'It's okay, mum,' I assured her. 'Looks worse than it is. Alby and me are just popping round to Derek Dickson's for a game of Monopoly. I've finished my homework. Won't be too long.' We were out of the door before she could ask any more questions.

At Dipper's we were joined by another of our Fourth Form pals, Tubbo Simms. Naturally the first thing they wanted to know was who had been trying to re-arrange my face.

'We've got a Great White Hope on our hands,' Alby announced, lifting my right hand like a referee declaring the winner at the end of a boxing match. 'Matt's just knocked Frankie Beckett out cold.'

'This one of your jokes, Alby?' said Tubbo.

'I kid you not,' said Alby. 'This very evening our mate laid out the mighty Beckett cold as a lump of North Sea cod.'

'Can we get on with the game,' I pleaded.

'Come on,' said Dipper, 'give us the real gen.'

I realised they wouldn't be satisfied until I explained what had happened, so I gave them a brief, unembellished account of the fight.

'Hate to be in your shoes,' said Dipper, after I'd finished. 'Frankie and the Sharkeys'll be gunning for you for sure.'

'Thanks for reminding me,' I said.

'I'd think about emigrating if I was you,' said Tubbo.

'They say Siberia's pretty in the winter,' said Dipper.

'Nah,' said Alby. 'Matt'll be all right. We'll think of something. Brains always beat brawn.'

'Is the condemned man allowed one last wish?' I asked.

'Go on then,' said Dipper.

'Can we please get on with the game?'

Alby suggested threepence apiece in the kitty. None of us really fancied our chances against him - we never did - but we agreed. He duly wheeled and dealed his way to ownership of Mayfair and Park Lane and several other properties, rapidly covering them with little red wooden hotels. Then he proceeded to strip us one by one of the meagre stock of properties and cash we had managed to acquire.

'Hard luck, lads,' said Alby as the last of us went bankrupt. He managed to sound genuinely sympathetic as he scooped up the coins in the kitty. 'Always a pleasure doing business with you gentlemen.' His grin exposed the gap between his incisors that was the envy of his contemporaries, not least because it enabled him to spit prodigious distances unattainable by anyone else in the school. It was an ability that won him many a bet.

As we walked home I asked Alby, not for the first time, how it was he almost always seemed to win when we played Monopoly or cards. He tapped the side of his nose and winked. 'I just work a little harder than the rest of you at being lucky.'

'You're the only person I know who never seems to have any bad luck,' I said.

The gap-toothed grin again. 'Some day I'll tell you how it works.'

'How about telling me now.'

'Time's not right.'

'When will it be?'

'Can't say,' said Alby, putting his arm around my shoulder, 'but when it is, you'll be the first to know. I promise you.'

As we reached the corner of Victoria Road, where Alby lived, he said, 'I'll call for you in the morning. Usual time.' Then he sauntered off, hands in his trouser pockets, whistling and kicking an imaginary football. I wondered how long he would go on treating life as a bit of a lark with him in the role of savvy observer.

CHAPTER FIVE

When a policeman turned up at our house the day after the fight with the news that Frankie Beckett was in hospital suffering from severe concussion, I though I was going to be arrested and charged with assault and battery or worse.

The constable seemed to read my mind. 'Don't worry,' he said, 'all we require from you at this stage is a statement of exactly what happened. Mr Beckett's mother told us he'd been involved in an altercation with you, but he couldn't remember much about it.'

'How is Frankie?' I asked.

'The doctors are always a bit wary about head injuries,' said the constable, 'but they reckon he should be okay in a few days.'

After the constable had written down my statement and I'd signed it, my mother, who had been listening intently to everything that had been said, addressed the policeman. 'I'm sorry about Frankie Beckett being hurt, but I hope you know the kind of person he is and the things he and his cronies get up to on this estate; thieving, bullying and goodness knows what else. I expect he'll be back to his old tricks as soon as he's recovered.'

'Don't worry Mrs Sheridan,' said the constable, 'Frankie and his associates are well known to the police.'

'They shouldn't be allowed to behave the way they do,' said my mother.

The PC nodded. 'We are aware of their activities, but we haven't been able to take any action against them because local people are too afraid to come forward and provide us with the hard evidence we need.'

After the policeman had left my mother said, 'I just pray to God Frankie won't feel he's got to get back at you.'

I'd been doing a little praying myself but I didn't let on.

Frankie was kept in hospital for four days and stayed off school until the following week. On his first morning back I was chatting to Alby in the playground when I spotted him, Lenny Bradd by his side, striding towards us.

'Play it calm,' Alby muttered as Frankie and Lenny approached.

Frankie came up close and looked me straight in the eye. 'I've been hearing stories,' he said, 'about you bragging you'd knocked seven kinds of shit out of me.'

'I've never told anybody I'd done that,' I said.

'You'd better give me the fucking truth,' said Frankie. 'All I know is I got a bang on my head and it blanked out my mind.'

'It was a pure accident,' I said.

He shook his head slowly. 'You're lucky I didn't kill you.'

Alby piped up, 'No, it was you who was lucky, Frankie'

Frankie stared at him. 'How d'you make that out, smart arse?'

'Simple,' said Alby. 'If you'd killed Matt you'd probably have got ten years for manslaughter, so him laying you out probably saved you from the slammer.'

Lenny Bradd grabbed Alby's tie and pulled him forward. 'You've got a big gob, Wilson.'

Frankie pushed his sidekick away from Alby. 'Leave it, Len. I'll sort out Sheridan when I'm good and ready. I want to do it properly; really enjoy it.'

As Frankie and Lenny walked off, Alby scratched his chin. 'How did a couple of numbskulls like that ever pass the eleven-plus?'

'Wish they hadn't,' I said. 'I don't fancy the idea of Frankie sorting me out, and enjoying it.'

'Don't fret, old son,' said Alby. 'Just remember you've got me in your corner.'

'I reckon I could do with Superman as well,' I said. I knew if it came to any kind of physical confrontation Alby and me would be no match for Frankie with or without his cronies.

Fine summer rain was beginning to sprinkle the playground as the bell rang and we headed for the science labs for a double lesson of Physics, and a morning to be spent exploring the intricacies of electricity and magnetism. Perhaps on another, happier day I might have shared something of the fascination the subject had apparently held for some gent called Michael Faraday. Instead I found my thoughts drifting elsewhere, to Outer Mongolia, Tasmania and other destinations far away from Frankie Beckett and the Sharkeys. When my mind headed homewards once more I got to wondering how much longer I would be the possessor of four fully functioning limbs and a complete set of teeth.

By the time we trudged out of the lab for the morning break, the rain had stopped and warm sunshine had already dried the playground surface.

'Glad that's over,' I said.

'What?' said Alby.

'All that electricity stuff. I wasn't in the mood for it this morning.'

'I love Faraday,' said Alby. 'Made more discoveries than you've had dripping sandwiches. Man after my own heart. Modest, really keen on the Big Fellah, and just wanted to be left in peace to change the world.'

'Exactly like you,' I said.

'Know what,' said Alby. 'Queen Victoria thought so much of old Mike she let him live in one her fancy apartments at Hampton Court.'

'How'd you know that?' I asked.

'Thornfield Public Library. I'm their best customer.' Alby glanced up at the cloudless sky. 'Looks like the Big Fellah's let us down. Every Wednesday afternoon this term it's been sun, sun and more bloody sun, right on cue. Not a single games afternoon, not one hour's cricket been rained off the whole season.'

As we strolled over to the school hall for lunch Alby went on grumbling. 'I thought we were safe when I woke up this morning; lovely dark clouds, a nice drizzle, then what happens? The Big Fellah decides to blow the clouds away and dries out the pitch just in time for the house match.'

For Alby, the excitement level of cricket lay somewhere between watching grass grow and paint dry. Nevertheless it had amused him to learn how to spin a cricket ball, and he became so proficient at it that he was the only kid in the school who could bowl a genuine googly. His skills were naturally in demand for school and house matches but, by employing various subterfuges, he

53

managed to dodge many of the games. His favourite ploy was to produce a doctor's note, which invariably referred to a mysterious recurring back condition. Once when I asked him how he was able to con the doctor into giving him notes for what we both knew was a totally fictitious ailment, he looked at me with mock horror. 'What me con the quack? Wouldn't dream of it.'

'How do you get the notes then?'

'Not too difficult,' said Alby. 'I was in our doc's surgery a while back having my adenoids looked at. He had to pop out of the room for something, so I just slipped a few sheets of his notepaper down my windjammer. Even for a quack his writing's terrible, but I've managed to forge it pretty well with a bit of practice.'

On the afternoons when they were excused games, holders of doctors' notes were normally sent to the school library for what was supposed to be extra work or revision. More often than not Alby used the time to study horse racing form in the Sporting Chronicle Handicap Guide, which he carefully concealed between the pages of an atlas. The school library just didn't have many of the kind of books Alby enjoyed reading; the sort he devoured during his visits to the Thornfield Public Library. His favourite subjects included astronomy, Greek mythology, great inventions and the lives of famous people. His special heroes were four gents he referred to as Len, Bill, Ike and Al. The library had plenty of books by and about them, shelved under their full names of   Leonardo da Vinci, William Shakespeare, Isaac Newton and Albert Einstein.

On this particular Wednesday afternoon Alby had been so convinced that the cricket would be rained off, he hadn't bothered to bring one of his doctor's notes. Thus he found himself joining me, Dipper Dickson and some of our other pals in the Greville House team to face the formidable eleven representing Tarleton House in a match that would decide the destination of the middle school cricket trophy for 1948.

By lunchtime the sun was defiantly in charge and Alby looked like he had swallowed a wasp. 'In future,' he said, as we headed for the sports field after school dinner, 'I'm going to keep a doctor's note in my desk for emergencies like today.'

When we got to the changing room most of the players from the two teams were already there. The Greville boys were huddled at one end and the Tarleton players at the other. A few lads were pulling on white flannels and shirts, but for most of us, changing for cricket meant simply taking off our blazers and ties and putting on a pair of pumps.

As our skipper Doug Grayson led the Greville team out into the sunshine he clapped his hands noiselessly and called, 'Come on lads, we can win this if we really get stuck in.' The expressions on the faces of his team members made clear his optimism was not shared. The thought of facing the awesome Tarleton bowling attack, spearheaded by Mick Golding, induced in all but the most courageous or foolhardy a feeling somewhere between apprehension and terror. Not only was Mick by far the school's fastest bowler, he was also its most unpredictable. Bouncers, wides, yorkers, bodyliners; no-one, least of all Mick, knew what was coming next, except that it would be quick. Bloody quick.

Our captain won the toss and put Tarleton in to bat first, which at least postponed the ordeal of facing Mick

Golding's bowling. While we waited in the sunshine for the Tarleton openers to arrive at the wicket, our skipper, perhaps reading our minds, tried once more to instil a little inspiration. 'Don't worry,' he said, 'Barney will clamp down on Golding if he starts slinging down any wild stuff.' Barney was the umpire, Guy Barnard, sometime all-rounder with the Warwickshire County second team and head of physical training at Herby's.

'Barney can't stop Mick slipping in the occasional bodyliner,' said Eddie Coates, our wicketkeeper, 'Mick'll just plead, as usual, that he accidentally lost control.'

'Oh for a doctor's note,' Alby whispered in my ear.

The game began more promisingly than we could have hoped with Nick Steadman, our one quickish bowler, bagging a couple of wickets early on. Then Doug Grayson called on Alby. His spinners bamboozled four middle order batsmen out before a defiant stand by the last wicket pair helped Tarleton to an eminently respectable total of 92.

As our openers, Eddie Coates and Dipper Dickson, strapped on their pads, Doug Grayson offered some last minute advice. 'Keep your eye on the ball, play a straight bat, and don't let Golding see you're scared.'

Watching Eddie and Dipper walk slowly to the middle, the only sound was the distant hum of traffic on Stackley Road, but I wouldn't have been surprised to have heard a lone trumpeter sounding *The Last Post*. Mick was pacing out his run-up, tossing the ball from hand to hand, as Dipper took his stance from Guy Barnard. On a signal from Barney, Mick began his run, accelerating with each stride, until he reached the wicket in a flurry of shirt sleeves and pounding feet. His right arm flashed over in a blur and an instant later the ball was skidding off the edge of

Dipper's pad into the gloves of the wicketkeeper. Mick and the 'keeper screamed for lbw, but Barney shook his head, giving Dipper the benefit of what must have been the slenderest of doubts.

Clearly miffed by the umpire's decision, Mick fired his next delivery wide as he strived for even more speed. The ball flew well beyond the wicketkeeper's reach and raced to the boundary for four extras. The third ball kept low and missed Dipper's leg stump by the thickness of a coat of varnish. Now Mick added five yards to his run and came thundering in like an express train making up for lost time. Such was the power of the delivery I could barely follow its flight, but I heard the dull thud as it crashed into the wicker box protecting Dipper's groin area. Practically the whole of the Tarleton team threw up their arms and yelled 'Howzat?'

'Bloody painful I should think,' Alby muttered, as the umpire raised his finger to signal the end of Dipper's brief innings. As he tottered back to the changing room, Alby shook his head. 'Poor old Dipper; of all people to be out GBW.'

'What's GBW?' asked Raymond Clegg.

'Goolies before wicket of course,' said Alby.

Raymond winced. 'Hope they've taken Golding off before I get in.'

The next six wickets fell for the addition of only 29 runs, most of which came
from extras conceded by Mick's more erratic deliveries. Doug Grayson was the only Greville player to score off Mick and was still there with 14 runs to his name when the seventh wicket fell. Alby was next in with myself and Raymond Clegg to follow.

57

As Alby sat on the boundary edge strapping on the pads just removed by the last batsman, he paused and stuck out a hand. 'Rain. I swear I can feel spots.'

We all looked skywards, and sure enough a murky grey canopy of cloud was forming overhead. The spots turned into splashes and soon the rain was coming down in stair-rods. Players, umpires and the small gaggle of Fourth Form spectators made a dash for the pavilion. As everyone crowded in, Guy Barnard tried to sound hopeful. 'Might be just a passing shower.'

'Please, Big Fellah,' Alby whispered, glancing heavenwards, 'keep the tap running.'

After half an hour, with the downpour showing no signs of letting up, Barney announced that the match would have to be postponed to the following Wednesday. Alby stood at the changing room window smiling up at the watery heavens. 'You left it late Big Fellah, but you came good in the end.'

'I expect you'll have a doctor's note for next week,' I said.

Alby grinned. 'I can feel the backache coming on already,' he said. 'I could do you a note as well if you like.'

'No thanks,' I said, 'I don't seem to live the kind of charmed life you do. I'd probably get rumbled straight away. Maybe you could ask the Big Fellah for more rain again next Wednesday.'

'Might be better if you ask him,' said Alby, nodding towards the streaming windows. 'This is the only rain I've been able to get out of him all season.'

Alby's suggestion reminded me that I was overdue for a chat with the Big Fellah. That night I asked him yet again if he could do something about my old man's

58

treatment of my mother, maybe instil just a modicum of common humanity in Frankie Beckett, and make me a little less awkward in the presence of girls, especially Helen O'Donnell. In exchange for a little help with any of those things, I told him, I wouldn't moan too much if he made the sun shine brightly next Wednesday afternoon and I had to face Mick Golding's bowling.   I never liked my chats with the Big Fellah to just consist of asking for favours though; I always tried to show a little gratitude for all the good things in my life. That night, not for the first time, I ended by thanking him for giving me a friend like Alby Wilson. Whatever the uncertainties in the days to come, the one thing I knew for sure was that I always felt better for having Alby around.

CHAPTER SIX

A hot, still Sunday afternoon. Alby and me were lying on our backs on the patch of lawn in his back garden watching the criss-crossing vapour trails created by a barely visible aeroplane high in the cloudless sky.

'Wonder who he is?' said Alby.

'Who?' I asked.

'The pilot of that kite up there.'

'What does it matter?'

'Might matter a lot.'

'Give me one good reason.'

Alby pondered a moment. 'He might have been a Spitfire pilot in the Battle of Britain.'

'So what if he was?'

'Could have shot down a German bomber that was just about to drop a thousand pounder on your house.'

'Come on, Alby.'

'If he had saved your house you'd be grateful to him, wouldn't you?'

'Yes, but…'

'How do we know he didn't win the Victoria Cross?' Alby sat up, his face animated. 'Just picture it. His Spit's riddled with bullets from a Messerschmidt 109, flames pouring out of his tail, his canopy shattered, he's bleeding like a tap from his wounds, but still he goes after the 109. There's a dogfight, up and down, round and round the sky, then the Spit loops the loop and comes out of the sun behind the Jerry, there's a splatter from his canons, and the 109 goes screaming down to earth and blows up in a big orange ball of flame.'

'Have you finished?' I asked, but he barely paused for breath.

'The Spit pilot starts to chase another 109, but his squadron leader sees how badly his kite's damaged and orders him back to base. He manages to nurse the crippled plane down onto the airfield as the fire engines and ambulance race across the runway to help. The ground crew cheer as the pilot climbs out of the cockpit with his face bloody and blackened by smoke. He's limping badly, but still manages to throw up a Churchill victory sign as they help him into the ambulance.'

'You read too many comics,' I said.

'They can be very educational,' said Alby.

We were both avid fans of such comics as *Wizard, Rover* and *Adventure,* but our favourite character was Rockfist Rogan, a fearless RAF squadron commander and boxer, whose adventures were featured each week in *The Champion.*

'That pilot making the smoke up there might never have been anywhere near the Battle of Britain,' I said. 'Could even be somebody on his first solo flight.'

'Don't you think you ought to give him the benefit of the doubt?' said Alby. 'I mean, you'd feel a bit of a twerp if we were in the snooker hall tonight and some bloke with a plummy voice and big twirly moustache strolls in and says, "Had a topping day chaps. Been putting the old kite through its paces. You might have noticed my vapour trails all over the sky, just like the ones we used to make when we were chasing those jerry fighters back in 1940."

61

I closed my eyes against the bright sun. 'Whatever you say, mate.'

'You give up too easily,' said Alby.

'I've learned from experience,' I said. 'No point wasting my breath when your brain goes off on one of its flights.'

Alby lay back silent for a few moments. 'Know what, I quite fancy the idea of joining the Air Force. Pair of big white wings on my chest. Flying Officer Albert Wilson DFC. Has a bit of ring to it, don't you think?'

'I thought you wanted to be a doctor,' I said.

'Yes, I did fancy it for a while. Think it was after seeing old Albert Schweitzer on the newsreel doing his stuff in Africa.'

'Albert who?'

'Schweitzer. You know, the bloke with the big droopy moustache and funny accent. Plays the organ and runs that hospital in the jungle. The natives think he's a saint.' Alby's face took on a wistful look. 'Come to think of it, I could quite take to the idea of being a saint. Don't believe we've ever had one in the family.'

I suggested sainthood might cramp his style somewhat. I doubted whether saints spent their school dinner money backing horses or forged doctor's notes to skive off cricket.

'Expect you're right,' said Alby.

I asked him why he'd gone off the idea of becoming a doctor.

'They reckon you need Latin to get into the quack colleges,' he said.

'You could handle it,' I said. 'You've never had any problem with French and German.'

Alby shook his head. 'Nah, I couldn't be bothered swotting up a dead lingo. And anyway I'm not sure I'd want to spend my time lancing boils and heating up piddle in test tubes.'

'I thought they got nurses to do the messy jobs,' I said.

'Not so sure about that,' said Alby. 'D'you know what a surgeon did to my Aunt Bessie last year?'

'No, what?'

'Cut off one of her tits.'

'Why did he do that?'

'It had some kind of disease in it.'

'She must have looked a bit lopsided in a sweater.'

'No,' said Alby, 'she stuffs the empty side of her bra with tissue paper. I heard her telling my mum.'

I said I was glad boys didn't have tits.

'Some do,' said Alby. 'What about Tubbo Simms? He's got a better pair than some of the girls in the Fourth.'

'His aren't real ones,' I said. 'They'd never be any good for feeding babies. They're just flab.'

'That's right,' said Alby. 'Girls' tits have lots of little tubes in them that fill up with milk when they have a nipper.'

'I know that,' I said.

'Did you know they're called mammary glands?'

'Of course,' I fibbed.

'And did you know they're erogenous zones?'

'What zones?'

'Never mind, but touching them there makes girls frisky.'

I said I thought girls had to fancy you before they let you touch them in those kind of places.

63

'Well yes,' said Alby, 'but if they do let you it makes them fancy you even more.Dipper Dickson's got a book that spells it all out with pictures and diagrams. Think he bought it at that second-hand bookshop on Stackley Road. Talking about touching girls, reminds me; how did you get on with Helen O'Donnell when you walked her home the other day?'

'We just talked.'

'What about?'

'This and that.'

'What kind of this and that?'

'Can't really remember.'

'Try.'

'Well… homework for one thing.'

'Is that all?'

'Not much else I can remember.'

Alby shook his head. 'You get the best looking dame in the Fourth Form all to yourself, and all you talk about is homework?'

'I didn't want to seem pushy.'

'You probably offended her.'

'How?'

'Girls might act all coy but they like to think blokes fancy them.'

'I do fancy her. A lot.'

'How's she supposed to know that if all you talk about is homework?'

'I didn't want to foul things up behaving like Errol Flynn or somebody.'

Alby nodded sagely. 'Okay, I'll grant you need to be a bit careful what you say with nice girls like Helen, but if you had to talk about school work you could at least have tried to get the conversation round to something like Human Biology. Dipper Dickson would disown you if he ever found out.'

'You won't tell him, will you?'

'Course not. Some things are for best mates' ears only.'

'And some things you shouldn't tell anyone,' I said. I didn't feel like sharing any more of my feelings about Helen, even with my best friend, so I decided it was time to change the subject. 'How'd you fancy a bike ride this afternoon?'

Alby thought for a moment. 'No, I've got a better idea, let's go for a swim in the cut. Too warm for riding bikes.'

'Yes, that's probably a better idea,' I agreed. The sun was getting hotter and the back of my shirt felt damp with sweat. Alby's pale face was a little flushed and beads of perspiration shone like tiny pearls on his forehead.

There was a clop clop of footsteps on the concrete path and Alby's mother appeared carrying two glasses of lemon squash. With an effort she bent her ample midriff and placed the drinks on the grass in front of us. 'There you are boys,' she said, 'and when you've drunk those I've got a little errand for you.'

'Matt and me were going to go swimming,' Alby protested.

'Not in that filthy canal again, I hope,' said Mrs Wilson. 'You could catch diphtheria.'

'Don't worry mum,' said Alby. 'We're careful not to swallow any water.'

Mrs Wilson shook her head in patient resignation.

'What was the errand?' Alby asked.

'I just wanted you to pop round to your gran's to collect some raspberries she's picked for us. Won't take you long.'

'Okay,' said Alby. 'Just hope gran isn't in one of her chatty moods.'

We downed the squash in a couple of long swigs. As we did so the vapour trails in the sky were slowly disintegrating like the feathers of some exotic bird.

Gran Ryder's house was in a terrace of tiny privately rented villas in a narrow cul de sac on the edge of the Thornfield estate. Alby had to rap on the polished brass knocker several times before the old lady came to the door.

She peered at us through pebble glasses perched on the end of her small snub nose and, as recognition dawned, she smiled, exposing the brown vulcanite gums of her false teeth. 'Alby me duck,' she said, planting a kiss full on his lips. 'How nice to see you. And you young Matthew.'

Like Alby's mum, her youngest daughter, Gran Ryder was short and stout, and on this day was wearing a bivouac of a frock that made her look like she was padded with pillows. Her chubby face, grey hair tied back in a bun, and the dark clothes she always wore put me in mind of the pictures I'd seen of Queen Victoria.

'You keeping all right, gran?' Alby asked.

'Not s'bad all things considered,' she said, as she ushered us along the dark hallway into the parlour. 'I'm the better for seeing you my love. Don't get a lot of visitors these days. Apart from your mum, of course. Haven't seen hide nor hair of your Aunt Win for nigh on five weeks.'

'Suppose it's a long way for her to come from Dudley,' said Alby.

Gran Ryder sniffed. 'She managed a week in

66

Bournemouth all right at Whitsun. And I hear she gets over pretty regular to visit that toffee-nosed sister-in-law of hers in Worcester.'

'Never mind, gran,' said Alby, putting an arm around her, 'we all think you're the world's best.'

The old lady's frown gave way to a smile. 'Suppose I'm not the jolliest of company these days, what with my rheumatism and bronchitis... oh just hark at me going on. Can I get you and Matthew a drink of something?'

'No thanks, gran,' said Alby, glancing at me for agreement, 'we had some squash before we came over. Mum said you had some raspberries for her.'

'Oh yes, a grand crop it's been this year. Real big beauties.' As she disappeared into her kitchen, Alby shook his head and grinned.

The old lady reappeared carrying a colander full of succulent looking raspberries. 'Take them in that,' she said, handing the container to Alby. 'Your mum can bring it back next time she comes over. And don't you go scoffing them all before you get home.'

'Don't worry, we'll save enough for a pie,' said Alby, as we turned to leave.

'You young rascal,' said Gran Ryder with a gummy smile. 'Give my love to your mum, and come and see me again soon.'

'Course I will,' said Alby, this time managing to avoid her proferred lips and kissing her on the cheek. 'And thanks for the raspberries.'

Once we had left the cul de sac, Alby chose one of the largest of the raspberries, tossed it high in the air, and caught it in his open mouth. 'Here,' he said, throwing one in my direction, 'try one.' I attempted to get my mouth

67

under it, but the raspberry caught the tip of my chin and splattered onto the pavement.

Alby laughed. 'You haven't got such a big gob as me,' he said as he spat raspberry pips like tracer bullets through the gap in his front teeth. 'Come on, let's get a spurt on, I'm dying for a swim.'

The chief attractions of the cut - aka the Grand Union Canal - was that, unlike the municipal baths, there was no admission charge and it never got crowded. We knew the factories upstream spewed in all sorts of chemicals and waste, but it didn't put us off. We assumed the pollutants floated to the bottom and seeped away in the mud. We tried not to swallow any water if we could help it, and always kept our eyes closed when we swam below the surface. Also we wore plimsolls and trod carefully on the canal bottom, which was a popular dumping place for old bike frames, broken washing mangles, weighted sacks of unwanted kittens, and anything else local folks needed to dispose of but was too big or illegal for the dustmen to collect.

Our favourite swimming spot was just below the GWR railway viaduct. Not many other kids ventured along that stretch because it involved an awkward climb down a steep gorse-covered embankment. On this Sunday afternoon we could hardly wait to get into the water. Undressing quickly, we put our clothes in a pile beneath a bush close to the edge and slipped into the canal. Soon we were floating on our backs in the pleasantly cool water.

After a while we heard the distant rumble of a Paddington express approaching. Suddenly it was directly above us on the viaduct, a roaring, clattering crescendo of noise. When the last carriage had passed from sight, we watched the iron bridge girders continuing to vibrate above us. Then the only sound was the gentle slap of water against the bridge abutments.

For some time we lay gently paddling our hands to stay afloat on the rippling water until we heard the phut phut of a barge heading our way. We swam to the side of the canal to watch. As it appeared round the bend in the canal we saw it was carrying a full load covered in tarpaulin, and at the stern a swarthy little man in a greasy cloth cap sat holding the rudder. The swell caused by the barge buffeted us as we stood thigh deep at the edge of the canal.

'What have you got under the covers?' Alby called to the bargee as the boat moved slowly by.

'That'd be telling,' said the man.

'Bet it's contraband,' said Alby, giving me a wink.

The bargee put a finger to his mouth. 'Shh, you'll get me locked up.'

'Go on, tell us what it is,' said Alby. 'We won't shop you.'

'Orl right then,' said the bargee as the boat chugged on, 'it's half a dozen cheeky young buggers like you I picked up along the side of the canal. I'm taking 'em down to Regents Park Zoo to be minced up for animal food.'

'Wish the animals bon appetit,' Alby shouted as the boat pulled away. Then he turned to me. 'I like those barge blokes; they're always good for a laugh.'

'What d'you reckon he was really carrying?' I said.

'Timber,' said Alby. 'Couldn't you see the tips of the planks sticking out from under the tarpaulin?'

After the barge had disappeared and the water calmed, Alby said, 'Come on, I'll race you across to the other side. You can have a yard start.'

'I'll take it,' I said, diving forward and heading across the canal as fast as my awkward crawl allowed. Alby drew level with me half way across, then stopped, treading water. 'What's that?' he said, pointing upstream just beyond the viaduct. Protruding from the thick mesh of rushes at the edge of the canal was what appeared to be a human foot. We paddled to the side and clambered out onto the towpath. 'Come on,' said Alby, 'we'd better take a look.'

My legs felt like jelly as we hurried along the towpath. I hardly dared contemplate what we might find. As we got close to the spot, Alby pulled aside the rushes, and there, floating face down in the shallow water, was the pallid, bloated body of a woman. Her yellow cotton dress had ridden up over her chest, exposing a whalebone corset with suspenders holding up dark stockings.

Alby's face had drained of colour and he looked like he might be sick any moment. I felt the same. Neither of us had seen a dead body before and we were frozen in numb silence for several moments. Then Alby muttered, 'You know who it is, don't you?'

I knew all right. We could see enough of her head and face to recognise Hetty Peck, the wife of Sid Peck, owner of the greengrocery shop on Stackley Road, the shop from which we had stolen pears just a few days ago.

'Come on,' said Alby, 'We need to get help.'

We dashed back along the bank to the spot where we'd climbed out of the water and swam across the canal as fast as we could to the place we had left our clothes. At any other time we would have lain in the sun to dry off before dressing, but now we gave our bodies a few cursory wipes with our towels and dressed as fast as we could. We were still pulling on our shirts as we scrambled up the embankment.

'We'd better head for the police station,' I said, as we reached the top.

'No,' said Alby, 'the Hare and Hounds is closer. They'll have a telephone.'

When we got to the pub, the landlord, Ted Goodwin, was just opening the doors for the Sunday lunchtime session.

'What's up lads?' he asked as we rushed up to the entrance of the public bar.

Breathlessly we told him what we had found.

'Come and sit down and get your breath back,' he said, 'and I'll phone the police.' As he did so a straggle of customers began drifting into the bar and the waft of cigarette smoke began overpowering the fresh carbolic smell from the overnight cleaning.

It wasn't long though before a traffic policeman arrived and we were soon on our way in a Wolseley patrol car back to the scene of our grisly discovery. The policeman parked the car near the viaduct and from the top of the embankment we were able to point out the spot where we had found Hetty Peck's body. Her corpse remained partially visible, bobbing gently in the shallow water near the rushes.

After the policeman had returned to the patrol car to radio for further assistance, Alby said, 'I wonder how long Hetty's been in the cut?'

'A while I should think by the look of her,' I said.

Alby nodded. 'I reckon so. Strange nobody spotted her before.'

'Maybe she was in the deeper water and her body's only just got washed up near the bank,' I ventured.

The policeman came back and told us to wait while he went down for a closer look at the body. As we watched him clamber down the embankment, Alby said, 'I've just ruled out policeman, pathologist, and canal superintendent from my career possibles list.'

Just then an ambulance drew up beside the police car and two men in green overalls emerged with a stretcher and what I took to be a canvas body bag. Alby directed them to the spot along the canal bank where the policeman was standing. 'Don't envy you the job of pulling her out of the water,' he said.

'All in a day's work for us,' said one of the ambulance men.

Watching them make their slithering descent to the canal, Alby said, 'You can add ambulance man to that career non-starter list.'

When the policeman returned, he asked us to go with him to the police station to make a statement. With the ink barely dry on my statement about my fight with Frankie Beckett, I reckoned I'd soon be getting as well-known to the local constabulary as the Sharkey gang.

Later, as were walking home, Alby said, 'Makes you think, doesn't it. While I was nicking those pears from her shop, poor old Hetty was probably already drowned in the cut.'

'I ate one of the pears,' I said, 'I'm just as guilty as you.'

'To be fair though,' said Alby, 'it was her old man we were pinching from, not Hetty.'

'Somehow that doesn't make me feel a whole lot better about it,' I said.

Glancing up at the sky, Alby whispered, 'About the pears, Hetty; it was nothing personal, honest. And we'll pay next time we have anything from your shop.'

I wasn't sure I ever wanted to go into Pecks' greengrocery again, but I knew we would have to come face to face with Sid Peck before too long. The police had informed us we would be required as witnesses at Hetty's inquest.

CHAPTER SEVEN

The inquest on Hetty Peck was held at the City Coroner's Court on a bright Wednesday afternoon in late June. Alby was delighted with the timing because it meant we missed not only the last lesson of the morning, which happened to be Scripture, but we also got out of an afternoon's cricket. For myself I wasn't so sure that a snooze through Scripture and quiet afternoon spent patrolling the fine leg boundary might not have been preferable to sitting in a courtroom listening to folk going over the gruesome details of Hetty's demise. Then I remembered the painful bruising I'd suffered facing Mick Golding's bowling in the replayed house match, and the drubbing our team received, and decided maybe the inquest had the edge over cricket after all.

Our classmates were mightily envious that we were to be witnesses in a case that was the biggest source of gossip on the Thornfield Estate since a curate at St Margaret's Church had got a barmaid from the Hare and Hounds pregnant. We milked our new celebrity by showing around the summonses we had received, which instructed us to appear before Her Majesty's Coroner, Ernest Stigwood LlB, at the City Coroner's Court 'to give evidence touching the death of Heather Margaret Peck', and warning that if we failed to appear we could be liable to a hefty fine. Alby certainly didn't need such a warning to ensure he attended. This was a completely new kind of experience, and he was always game for one of those.

We got the bus into the city centre and arrived at the court building nearly an hour before Hetty's inquest was due to begin. Another inquest was in progress so we sat on one of the long oak benches in the lobby and played chess with Alby's pocket set while we waited. We were well into the game before a few other people drifted in and sat down on the benches around us. Sid Peck was the only one of them we knew, but if he recognised us, he showed no sign of doing so. By the time the usher called us into the court promptly at two thirty, we had abandoned the chess game to watch the comings and goings in the lobby.

Neither Alby nor I knew quite what to expect as we entered the hushed oak-panelled courtroom. Our impressions of what happened in such places was derived mainly from Hollywood films. The reality turned out to be a touch less dramatic. Apart from Alby and me and Sid Peck, the only people in the room were a tall gaunt man in a black jacket and grey striped trousers, three policemen, a bored looking young woman sitting at what I assumed was the press bench, and an elderly tramp dozing in the back row of the seats at the rear of the courtroom.

Sid Peck, wearing a sober double-breasted navy blue suit and black tie, was standing a few feet away from us deep in conversation with the tall gaunt man, who was clutching a thick manilla folder tied with pink tape.

'That'll be Sid's solicitor,' said Alby.

'I'd already worked that out,' I said.

Alby grinned. 'Course you had.'

'Sid looks different in that smart suit,' I said. 'I've only ever seen him in the cow gown he wears in the shop.'

'Looks every inch a Tory councillor doesn't he?' said Alby.

I didn't argue although I wasn't sure how you distinguished a Tory councillor from anyone else who happened to be wearing a smart suit.

Alby whispered in my ear, 'Bet he paid an arm and a leg for that outfit, made to measure of course. Mind you, he could have done with a couple of coat sizes bigger.'

Looking at Sid's bulging midriff I had to agree.

'It's all those free banquets and booze-ups councillors go to,' said Alby.'

'Tory councillor or not, you've got to feel sorry for him today,' I said.

'Course I do,' said Alby, 'but I feel even sorrier for Hetty.'

'All stand!' The voice of the court usher signalled the entrance of the coroner. Mr Stigwood took his seat, and cast his eye over the sparse gathering before him. Brisk but softly spoken, he blinked over his gold spectacles and explained in meticulous detail the purpose of the inquest. The snoozing tramp was probably the only person in the room who was not already well aware why we were all there.

Sid Peck was the first witness called. As he shuffled to the witness box, Alby whispered in my ear, 'First time I've ever pitied a Tory.'

Sid stared straight ahead as he took the oath in a barely audible voice and confirmed he was the husband of the late Heather Margaret Peck, known as Hetty. In answer to questions from the Coroner, Sid told of identifying her body at the city mortuary, and how he had noticed nothing in her behaviour in the days before her death to suggest her state of mind might be suicidal, although she had seemed a little quieter and more withdrawn than usual. It wasn't until he found her note the day she disappeared that he realised what was going on in her mind. When Mr Stigwood said the contents of the note would be   reported later in police evidence Sid winced and looked down at his feet.

After a few more routine questions about Hetty's movements in the days before her disappearance, Sid was followed in the witness box by the pathologist, Professor somebody or other, who had carried out a post-mortem on Hetty. His brusque matter-of-fact manner made me think of a bored waiter reiterating for the umpteenth time the specials on a dinner menu. He spared no lurid detail in describing the contents of Hetty's stomach, lungs and oesophagus, and telling us of her swollen brain, the haemorrhaging in her middle ear, and various other unpleasant results of being submerged for a long time in water.

Alby, curious as always, had spent time at the Thornfield Library reading up on the effects of drowning, so he knew the meaning of most of the clinical terms used by the pathologist . Among the results of his enquiries, which Alby passed on to me with no little relish, were that after three minutes under water you become unconscious, a couple of minutes after that you suffer brain damage, and then your heart stops. You actually die of suffocation. We both decided that, apart from being burned at the stake, drowning would be our least favoured way of dying.

I was trying to imagine what could have made Hetty desperate enough to drown herself   when Alby whispered, 'I think one of us will be called up next. Don't be nervous.'

The coroner thanked the pathologist with what seemed excessive graciousness for his contribution, then called for Albert Wilson to go into the witness box. Alby strode forward and took the oath like it was something he did regularly.

'Just tell the court in your own words what you witnessed on that Sunday afternoon when…' Mr Stigwood's words were interrupted by the sound of snoring from the back of the court. The tramp was lying back in his seat, head slumped forward on his chest, his mouth hanging open like a crane bucket. The Coroner gestured to his usher to wake the sleeper. When quiet was restored, Mr Stigwood turned once more to Alby. 'Forgive the interruption, Mr Wilson. Please continue.'

Alby reiterated the facts we had given the police in our statements and when he'd finished the Coroner told him his evidence had been exceptionally clear and helpful. The Coroner asked me if there was anything I wanted to add to Alby's testimony, and I told him I thought my friend had covered everything I would have said.

The constable who had accompanied Alby and me to the spot where we found Hetty's body gave his evidence and then the police inspector in overall charge of the case presented the bit of evidence Alby and me had been awaiting with huge curiosity - the note left by Hetty Peck, designated by the Coroner as Exhibit A.

As the   inspector read out Hetty's words in a slow monotone I watched the expression on Sid Peck's face change from drawn to grim:

Dear Sid,

By the time you read this it will be all over. I shall be at peace and you will be free to be with the young woman you apparently want. Yes, I have known about your affair with Lucy Simmons for quite a while, but I foolishly hoped it was a passing

78

thing, a middle aged man having his head turned by a pretty girl. I now realise it has gone on too long for that. I always tried to be the kind of wife I thought would make you happy, but it seems that despite all those good years together, I failed. I hope you will find what you are looking for with Miss Simmons. I am sorry if what I am going to do upsets those I love and who care about me. I ask their forgiveness and hope they will understand.

Your ever faithful wife,
Hetty

Alby and me exchanged glances. 'So all those rumours about Sid having it off with Lucy Simmons are true,' I whispered. 'Poor old Hetty.'

. For the first time the young woman on the press bench looked interested in the proceedings and was scribbling furiously in her notebook. Soon the whole community would be gossiping about how Hetty Peck had been driven to suicide by her husband's affair with Lucy Simmons.

The Coroner summed up the evidence in a careful, detached manner and concluded that Hetty had taken her own life while the balance of her mind was disturbed

'Know what,' said Alby as we went to catch the bus home, 'I don't feel so bad now about nicking those pears from Sid Peck.'

CHAPTER EIGHT

After the Hetty Peck episode, the canal lost its attraction for Alby and me. On the rare occasions we could afford the entrance charge we indulged our continuing keenness for swimming with visits to the municipal baths. It was as we were on our way home from there one Saturday afternoon that Alby spotted a notice in the window of Spicers' Newsagents advertising for newspaper delivery boys.

'What do you think?' he said.

'The cash would be handy,' I said.

'Yes,' said Alby, 'we could go to the baths a lot more, and the snooker hall. But even better, Lucy Simmons works at Spicers. We could get to know her, and maybe find out what she's really like and what she's been up to with Sid Peck.'

'I wouldn't have though she'd want to gossip about that,' I said.

'We'll see,' said Alby. 'Come on, let's go and find out what Mr Spicer's got to offer.'

We were disappointed to find Lucy Simmons wasn't in the shop, and Alby asked as casually as he could if she still worked there. Mr Spicer explained she had Saturdays off. We had no trouble getting taken on as delivery boys, thanks to Alby's charm and my willingness, albeit reluctant, to accept one of the longer paper rounds.

We soon came to enjoy our new found affluence, though our pleasure diminished a little when our paths crossed with lads delivering for Gillmans, the newsagents at the more affluent end of Stackley Road near Chamberlain Park, and we discovered that they were paid sixpence a week more than us. We consoled ourselves with the knowledge that Gillmans didn't have the added attraction of Lucy Simmons behind their counter.

Each afternoon after school we could hardly wait to get to Spicers' to pick up the newspapers for our rounds because it was usually Lucy who counted them out for us to put them in our delivery bags. We would watch her, fascinated, wondering how many of the more salacious rumours about her were true. Did she really allow lads a fumble for a tanner and let blokes go all the way for half a crown? Eddie Coates swore his older brother, Sam, had seen her going at it with a sailor in broad daylight in the quiet corner of Chamberlain Park known as Shag Alley.

Whenever Lucy's name came up in conversation among our school pals, someone was likely to launch into a ditty that began:

'Down in the valley where nobody knows
There lives a lady without any clothes,
Charges big fat men two pound ten,
Nippers six a penny...'

The better we got to know Lucy though, the harder we found it to believe the stories about her. She seemed such a pleasant, good-natured girl, too nice to offer her favours for cash. Anyway, we reasoned, if her affair with Sid Peck was as serious as Hetty had believed, she probably wouldn't be having it off with all and sundry any more, even if she had been before. Nevertheless our curiosity remained keen and Alby rarely missed a chance to do a little subtle probing.

'Do anything interesting last night, Luce?' he asked

81

her one afternoon as she was counting out his papers.

'None of your business, Alby,' she said without looking up.

'Just showing a friendly interest,' said Alby.

'You're being nosey more like,' she said.

A look of injured innocence spread over Alby's face. 'What me? You've really hurt me now Luce.'

'Well, if you must know,' she said, 'I went to the pictures.'

'What was on?'

'The Red Shoes.'

'What's that about?'

'A ballet dancer.'

'Sounds boring.'

'Not if you like ballet.'

'Do you?'

'It's okay.'

'Who'd you go with?'

'You're being nosey again.'

'Why the mystery, Luce?'

'There's no mystery,' she said, her face reddening, 'I went with a friend.'

'A bloke.'

'Yes, a gentleman. So what?'

'He wouldn't happen to own a greengrocery shop by any chance?'

'Alby Wilson you've got the cheek of the devil.'

'Only teasing, Luce,' said Alby. 'It's a free country; you can go to the pictures with anybody you fancy. Even greengrocers.'

'One of these days Alby Wilson, I swear I'll…'
Before she could finish, Alby had grabbed his bag and was

out of the shop.

Lucy turned to me with a faint smile. 'If I wasn't so fond of your pal, I'd give him a clip round the ear,' she said.

That night it was Alby's turn to have Dipper Dickson, Tubbo Simms and me round to his house for a card session. When I arrived Mrs Wilson opened the door and welcomed me with the familiar warm smile that put deep dimples into her chubby cheeks. 'Nora and Frank are here,' she said. 'They've popped in to let us see their new baby.'

Alby's cousin Nora and her husband Frank were sitting on the settee with Alby beside them holding the baby on his lap. His forced smile couldn't hide his discomfort.

After the ritual pleasantries, Nora and Frank turned back to gaze adoringly at their new offspring. 'Our Alby's ever so good with little Arnold,' cooed Nora. 'And you can tell Arnold loves him.'

'You certainly can,' I enthused.

'Alby will make a lovely daddy some day,' said Nora.

'I think Arnold's doing something in his nappy,' said Alby, avoiding my gaze.

'Ahh, the little love,' said Nora. 'Here, I'll take him.'

Alby handed the pungent, red-faced bundle to its mother, then glanced in my direction, lifting his eyes skywards.

Nora held Arnold up and sniffed his bottom, then nodded with a smile. She laid him on the floor and was rifling round in a bag for a clean nappy when Dipper and Tubbo arrived together. Dipper, never renowned for his tact, held his nose and said, 'Blimey, somebody's been on the baked beans.'

Alby stood up and turned to his mother, who had been watching the proceedings with faintly disguised amusement. 'All right if we play cards in the kitchen, mum?'

'Well, I was planning to do some baking,' she said.

'That's okay,' said Alby, 'we can play in the shelter.'

'You sure?' said Mrs Wilson, 'it's damp down there.'

'It'll be fine,' said Alby. 'We've used it before.'

We said our farewells to Nora and Frank and headed for the Anderson air raid shelter at the bottom of the Wilsons' back garden. Alby pulled open the rotting plywood door and climbed down the steps into the dark interior. He switched on the single electric light bulb suspended on a short wire from the metal ceiling. As the rest of us stepped down into the cramped chamber, dampness seemed to hang in the air. Trickles of condensation ran down the corrugated metal walls, creating glistening little puddles on the concrete floor.

'When's your old man going to dig up this tin box, Alb?' Dipper asked. 'War's been over three years. It'll soon be the last shelter left on the estate.'

'My dad's quite fond of the rockery up on top,' said Alby. 'And you never know, it might come in useful again. The way things are looking we could end up going to war with the Russkies and their Commie chums.'

'These little toffee cans wouldn't be a fat lot of use

84

if we did,' said Tubbo. 'Not with atom bombs flying around.'

'Anyway,' said Alby, 'it's better than nothing for a game of cards. We can sort out the future of the world later.'

We sat down on the upturned fruit boxes arranged around a small folding table and Alby took out a well-worn pack of cards from his a pocket. After shuffling them like a casino pro he placed them in the middle of the table. 'A few hands of Pontoon to start off?' he asked.

We mumbled our assent and each of us drew a card to decide who should occupy the role of banker. Tubbo and I picked up low cards, but Dipper drew an ace of diamonds, only to be matched by another ace drawn by Alby, this time a spade.

'Hard luck Dip,' said Alby. 'Spades is the top suit.'

Dipper frowned. 'Who says so?'

Alby smiled patiently. 'Ask any Bridge player. Spades takes it.'

'But we're playing Pontoon,' protested Dipper.

'You take your lead from Bridge,' said Alby. 'It's the main game, the one the nobs play.'

'Bugger the nobs,' said Dipper.

'Alright,' said Alby, 'I always believe in keeping the punters happy. We'll draw again.'

This time Dipper picked up a seven, Tubbo was only one higher, and I drew the queen of hearts. Alby smiled and shook his head apologetically as he held up the king of clubs.

After several rounds in which the banker's pile of pennies and threepenny bits rose steadily the rest of us watched ours shrink correspondingly, Alby suggested a switch to Brag. 'Give you guys a chance to change your luck,' he said.

Fortunes fluctuated in the new game, but Alby's pile remained undiminished and, at his suggestion, we finished with a few hands of the fast gambling game Shoot. By the end I had fivepence left, Tubbo was cleaned out and Dipper owed Alby a shilling and threepence.

'Tell you what, Alb,' said Dipper, reaching inside his coat and pulling out a copy of *Lilliput,* 'You can have this and call it quits if you like.'

Alby thumbed through the magazine, pausing at the pages displaying nude women, before finally holding it open at a page on which a shapely blonde was kneeling on a sheepskin rug. He asked Tubbo and me what we thought of Dipper's proposition.

'I'd rather have the cash,' said Tubbo. 'Buy you a nice fish and chip supper.'

I said I was inclined to share Tubbo's sentiment.

'Trouble with those *Lilliput* pictures,' said Alby, 'they paint out all the interesting bits.'

'You have to use your imagination,' said Dipper.

'I've got an idea,' said Alby, shuffling the cards and spreading them across the table. 'Why don't we draw for double or quits?'

Dipper hesitated, then withdrew a card. Alby did the same. Dipper held up the ten of hearts and Alby the eight of clubs.

'You win, Dip,' said Alby. 'Now we're quits.'

As Dipper wiped an imaginary spot of sweat from his forehead, Alby turned to me and winked. I had no doubt he knew before he chose it which card he was picking up.

As we climbed out of the air raid shelter the night

air was nippy and the red-tinged sky was blanketed with stars. 'Looks like it's going to be a nice day for our Enid's wedding tomorrow,' said Alby.

I wasn't keen on weddings but I liked Alby's sister Enid, and he had already talked me into going with the promise that 'there'll be some great crumpet, and the grub shouldn't be bad either.'

As we said our farewells I was almost looking forward to the morning.

CHAPTER NINE

The hall of Palmerston Lane Junior Mixed School was the only place on the Thornfield estate with sufficient space to accommodate proper celebrations for the more important rites of passage like wakes, bar mitzvahs and wedding receptions. It was also renowned for its unforgettable odour, a mingling of floor polish, sweat and stewed cabbage.

On the Saturday morning of Enid's wedding Alby and me, his dad and two of his uncles arrived early to set up the long trestle tables for use at the reception and sit-down meal.

'Blimey,' said Alby's Uncle Wally as we stepped into the hall, 'the pong's just as bad as it was when I was a nipper here forty years ago.'

'It's impregnated in the walls and the floors,' said Alby's Uncle Bill.

'Our Enid's bought some scented stuff to spray around before the do,' said Mr Wilson. 'Trouble is it'll probably make the place stink like a poof's parlour.'

'Think I'd rather put up with the old familiar niff,' said Uncle Wally.

After we had helped put up the tables, Alby and me drifted into the adjacent school kitchen where Gran Ryder and her two daughters, Alby's Aunts Bessie and Win, were making sandwiches. Gran Ryder and Aunt Bessie were slicing up white tin loaves while Aunt Win spread the slices with a mixture of margarine and butter. Then the three of them, hardly pausing for breath as they chattered, made mounds of little triangular sandwiches filled with either cheese and brown pickle or bloater paste and cucumber. These were piled onto several large oval plates and covered with tea towels to keep off the flies. Next the women set about washing and chopping lettuces, tomatoes, spring onions and radishes and placing them in glass bowls.

Meanwhile Alby's dad and the uncles were covering the tables with white lining paper, which they secured with drawing pins. When that was completed, Gran Ryder and the aunts began laying out the crockery and cutlery, most of it borrowed from relatives and neighbours. They placed the bowls of salad at strategic intervals along the tables and beside them little groupings of bakelite cruets, jars of pickled onions, piccalilli and salad cream. The sandwiches were then brought in from the kitchen, along with bowls of sherry trifle and jelly and blancmange, after which the women went up and down the tables with trays of boiled ham, ox tongue and brisket, placing a slice of each on the plates. Finally the two-tier wedding cake made by Alby's mother was brought in and placed in the centre of the top table.

The men carried in crates of brown ale, stout and lemonade and two large casks of mild ale, which had been collected from the outdoor at the Hare and Hounds the night before in Uncle Bill's Jowett. A plentiful supply of bottles and glasses was placed along the tables and the crates of spares booze left on the floor at the end of each table.

'I could just knock back one of them,' said Uncle Wally eyeing the bottles he had helped bring in.

'Isn't time,' said Alby's dad. 'We've got to go

home and change into our glad rags and get ourselves to the church.'

'Whatever you say, Cliff,' said Uncle Wally, but he didn't look best pleased.

All of us, except Aunt Win, trooped out of the hall. She had volunteered to miss the wedding service so she could be at the school hall ahead of the other guests to make sure everything was ready, and to spray the hall with the air freshener Enid had provided.

As Alby and me walked home I said I would have volunteered to miss the service instead of Aunt Win if I'd known someone was needed. I was sure a doting aunt would have enjoyed Enid's big moment even more than me.

Alby shook his head. 'Not Aunt Win. She's got no time for churches and reverend gents.'

'How's that?' I asked.

'Something that happened when she was a kid,' said Alby. 'A randy vicar. From what I've picked up over the years, seems that while she was attending confirmation classes, the rev. was putting his hand where he shouldn't have done. Frightened the life out of her, and put her off religion for good.'

The sky was a muddy yellow-grey as I arrived at St Margaret's Church, and the murk made the unlovely building look even grimmer than usual. The guilty thought occurred to me that maybe it was a pity the aerial torpedo that hit the place in 1942, the same night a German bomb landed on Herby's, hadn't done a more efficient demolition job. As it was, the only part of the church that had been damaged had been rebuilt using salvaged bricks to restore the place almost to its original look.

I managed to find a seat in a pew near the back of the church. It was occupied by two elderly couples, who I recognised as being from the Thornfield estate, though I didn't know their names. They smiled as I sat down. I bowed my head, not so much in prayer, but to avoid having to make small talk, which I always found difficult.

As we waited for the bride to arrive, I tried to concentrate my mind on pious thoughts, but was too conscious of the discomfort in my buttocks on the hard wooden pew. Despite this, and the efforts of the organist, who seemed to be doing his best to entertain the congregation with some lively, if unfamiliar, tunes, I found myself stifling yawns. The card session the night before had gone on rather late.

Alby, sitting up front between his mother and Aunt Bessie, looked like he too was having trouble remaining conscious. His head kept drooping forward and he would then jerk it up again and shake it.

With the minutes ticking away, I wondered if perhaps Enid had changed her mind about marrying her fiancé, Stan Ballard, a travelling salesman for a ladies underwear firm. Alby called him Stan the Spiv because of his sidelines buying and selling motor cycles, vacuum cleaners, radios and anything else he could lay his hands on to turn a profit. I found myself beginning to hope Enid had come to her senses and done a runner. Then I remembered brides are supposed to turn up late so as not to seem too desperate to land their chap. Anyway, Enid was much too kind-hearted to leave a bloke in the lurch, even a twerp like Stan.

While we waited I had a good look at the bridegroom's family and friends on the other side of the aisle. Noisily chattering among themselves, most of the women were wearing outfits my mother would have classified as tarty. The men sported mainly serge or striped suits, though some of the younger ones had opted for flashier gabardine.

In one of the pews near the back I spotted a young woman wearing a shiny silver sheaf dress with a neckline that plunged to a depth that would have tested the good intentions of a Trappist monk. I tried closing my eyes and thinking of depressing things like Woodwork lessons and toad-in-the-hole and Frankie Beckett, but couldn't stop myself snatching glances at the girl in silver. Each time she seemed to be smiling in my direction. Could she really be trying to get off with me? My recent bout of acne had almost cleared up and the crew cut I'd had on an impulse had nearly grown out, so I was feeling a little more presentable than of late.

By the time the organist struck up with *Here Comes the Bride* and Enid and her dad had gone by with a rustle and nervous smiles, I had almost managed to stop myself sneaking glances at Miss Silver and was keeping my head facing the altar. A few rows in front I noticed Gus Ryder, Alby's cousin, wearing his army uniform with a single lance-corporal's stripe on each arm blancoed to a dazzling white. He winked and smiled. I nodded back, but then realised it wasn't me he was looking at but someone beyond me. I glanced round to see the girl in silver returning his smile and nodding. I felt a flush of embarrassment run up my neck and inflame my cheeks. To hell with her, I decided; let her have Gus and his uniform and his blancoed stripes if that's what she wanted. Wasn't it loose women who always went for uniforms, anyway?

But it was no use, I couldn't suppress my envy of Gus. I resolved that if I could summon up enough courage, I would ask Miss Silver for a dance at the reception. I'd have to wait for a waltz though; that was the only dance for which I knew any steps. I'd learned them from Alby, who had been coerced by Enid into acting as her partner while she practised to strict tempo Victor Sylvester records. Alby and me thought dancing was a bit poofy, but decided to give it a go after Dipper Dickson's older brother Howard assured us that a little ballroom know-how was the next best thing to an MG open-topped tourer for pulling girls.

Apart from Miss Silver's presence, the only entertaining diversion occurred during the exchanging of rings when someone in the congregation unleashed a rippling fart. The scathing look I saw Aunt Bessie giving Uncle Wally left no doubt as to the identity of the culprit. Despite the stifled giggles and the sulphurous odour drifing across the pews, the Reverend Trittiford didn't even twitch a nostril as he discharged his sacramental duties. The verger, sitting beside the church entrance, seemed equally oblivious as he busied himself with the dual tasks of picking his nose and solving the Daily Mirror crossword.

It came as a blessed relief when we finally trooped out into the dank greyness of the English summer afternoon. Standing among the gnarled oaks and crumbling gravestones, the women dabbed their eyes and cooed about how moving the service had been and how lovely the bride looked, while the men grumbled about missing the Blues' match or their customary session at the pub, or did a lot of guffawing about nothing in particular.

Alby was showing me where his Grandad Ryder was buried when Gran Ryder came over. 'Turning in his grave I shouldn't wonder,' she said.

'Why's that, gran? asked Alby.

'Our Enid marrying that Stan Ballard.'

'Could've been worse,' said Alby. 'Even Stan's an improvement on that poncy hairdresser Enid was stuck on before.'

The old lady frowned. 'That's as may be, but I wouldn't give Stan Ballard houseroom. Smarmy as they come, never looks you in the eye. I suppose it's not surprising from a ladies underwear salesman.'

Alby winked at me. 'Yes, a bloke travelling in frilly knickers is a bit worrying.'

'You know what I mean, Alby,' said Gran Ryder, waving a stubby finger.

He grinned. 'Yes, I know what you mean, gran.'

Dark clouds were gathering as the photographer took the obligatory pictures of the bride and groom and the immediate relatives. Then, as he was lining up the guests for a large group shot, the rain came down, steadily at first, then with plant flattening ferocity. Guests dutifully remained in place long enough to have their kamikaze smiles and dripping wedding outfits recorded for posterity, then set off in a stampede to the waiting cars lined up outside the churchyard gate. Some were able to squeeze into one of the official vehicles with the bride and groom's families, a few had their own cars, but most headed for the shelter across the road to wait for the next bus that would take them to Palmerston Lane School. Among the crush in the shelter I glimpsed Aunt Bessie and Uncle Wally. She looked close to tears as she held on to her large feathered hat, now turned into a floppy sou'wester, while her husband was forlornly wiping his bald pate with a handkerchief. A few guests with umbrellas started walking to the school, a distance of   nearly a mile, if you knew the short-cut   across the Thornfield estate.

Alby and me ignored the rush to the cars and decided, since we were already drenched, we might as well walk to the reception We had gone about half way when Alby said, 'Come on, I'll race you.' As we ran the rain turned to hail and pummelled our faces, and the puddles on the pavement soaked our trousers and socks. I reached the school gates several yards ahead of Alby, the first time I'd beaten him in one of our occasional ad hoc races. I turned round to tease him, but saw he was leaning against the playground railings grimacing.

'   You all right, Alb?' I asked.

He stood gasping for a several moments. 'Came over a bit peculiar,' he said.

'You don't look too brilliant,' I said.

'I'll be fine in a minute,' he said. 'Of course I could've won, but I reckoned it was time I gave you a bit of encouragement.'

'Sure you did,' I said. 'Come on, let's go and get dried off.'

In the boys' lavatories we took off our shoes and squeezed the water from our socks. Then we dried our hair and faces on the roller towels. Other guests were coming in to do the same as we headed for the school hall to join the party.

Alby had arranged for us to sit together on one of the tables reserved for the younger guests. Seated opposite us was Gus Ryder, and beside him, the girl in the silver dress. As we introduced ourselves I felt myself flushing. The girl was called Sheila.

'What d'you do for a living, Sheila?' Gus wanted to know.

'I'm a typist,' she said.

'What d'you type?'

'Sales reports mostly,' she said.

'Sounds like a load of laughs.'

'Oh it is.'

'Know what, darling,' said Gus. 'You're wasting your talent in the typing pool; you ought to be one of them fashion models.'

Sheila beamed. 'Do you think so?'

'Definitely,' said Gus, ogling her neckline. 'I can see you now on the front page of one of them glossy women's magazines.'

Alby nudged me and whispered, 'Isn't he a pain in the backside.'

'You look petty smart yourself in your uniform, Gus,' purred Sheila. 'What d'you do in the army?'

'Can't really talk about it,' said Gus. 'It's hush hush. Involves working behind enemy lines, that sort of thing.'

'I didn't think we had any enemies now the war's over,' said Sheila.

'That's what the government like people to believe,' said Gus. 'You'd be surprised how many enemies we've got out there. It's specially trained soldiers like me who have to sort them out.'

Gran Ryder seated at the next table had evidently been listening in to Gus's conversation with Sheila. 'You're in the Pioneer Corps, aren't you, Gus?' she said.

'That's right, gran,' he said, pointing to his shoulder flashes.

96

'I though they spent most of their time digging latrines and doing labouring jobs.'

Gus shook his head. 'Just a wicked rumour. We're the ones they send for when there's special jobs to be done that ordinary soldiers can't handle.'

'Pull the other one, Gus,' said Gran Ryder. 'Anyway you peacetime soldiers don't know you're born. Ernie Blake, my next-door neighbour, was on the Russian convoys. Torpedoed twice. The last time he lost four of his toes with frostbite after they pulled him out of the Arctic.'

'Nasty,' said Sheila. 'I hate the cold.'

'Don't worry love,' oiled Gus, 'I'll keep you warm.'

Sheila giggled.

Gran Ryder took a swig from her glasss of Mackeson stout and eyed Gus steadily. 'Some of Ernie's shipmates lost their wotsits to the frostbite. Just shrivelled up and went black.'

'Blimey,' said Gus, glancing groinwards.

'Bet you're glad you're in the army and not the navy,' said Alby.

Gus looked thoughtful.

Sheila glanced across at Alby. 'And what does the bride's brother want to do when he leaves school?'

'He can't make up his mind between being a secret agent and a latrine digger,' said Alby.

Sheila giggled, but Gus looked like he could have strangled Alby.

At the top table Enid was nursing a glass of sparkling wine and glancing nervously around at the guests as they waded into the food and the booze. The best man, one of Stan's fellow salesmen called Vic, seemed to be sinking more ale than most. Eventually he rose, swaying gently, and stood looking about with a vacant grin on his face until the bridegroom whispered something in his ear. Then, slow and slurred, he began reading out the telegrams. With frequent pauses for swigs of brown ale, Vic stumbled through the required thank yous, leered at Enid's maid of honour, and finished by fouling up the punchline of a joke about the rev count of a homosexual bishop who happened to be a car enthusiast.

Alby's dad, also by this stage well lubricated, delivered a rambling, sentimental speech, out of character with his usual dry humour. He portrayed Enid as having a range of saintly qualities unequalled in the history of womankind, but had much less to say about his new son-in-law. He did, though, get a laugh from the male guests when he pointed out that Stan knew more about women's knickers than any other man in the room. Mrs Wilson stared into her lap and Enid's cheeks turned the colour of beetroot.

When Cliff Wilson finally sat down, Alby said, 'I never heard my dad rabbit on like that before.'

'Probably because he's not used to making speeches,' I suggested.

'He should be,' said Alby, 'he's a shop steward.'

Gus grinned. 'He probably isn't usually pissed at union meetings.'

'I think Mr Wilson's sweet,' said Sheila. 'You could tell he was speaking from the heart.'

There was tangible relief all round when, the cake cutting ritual completed, Gran Ryder and some of Alby's other female relatives began clearing the tables and removing the dirty crockery and what little remained of the food to the kitchen. After an hour and a half on folding wooden chairs, it meant legs could be stretched, bottoms discreetly massaged and bladders relieved.

The men stacked most of the trestle tables at one end of the hall, leaving just one standing to act as a bar, on which the booze supplies were stacked. Chairs and benches were placed around the perimeter of the hall, and Enid's relatives and friends arranged themselves along one side, Stan's along the other. For a while the opposite camps sat talking among themselves, eyeing each other suspiciously across the no-man's land that divided them. Eventually some of the younger children from the Wilson side began a game of tag and, hesitatingly at first, kids from the other side joined in. But it wasn't until Aunt Bessie squeezed her ample buttocks onto the piano stool and started thumping out her repertoire of popular songs, that the party really began to warm up.

Enid didn't look too keen to be first on the dance floor, but Stan hooked his arm through hers and hauled her on. They were quickly followed by Gus and Sheila, and soon the hall was a seething, noisy crush of young and old set on making a night of it. Aunt Bessie's honky-tonk style soon had the throng singing as well as dancing. When Uncle Wally insisted on doing his party piece, a rendering of *Galway Bay* in an excruciating Irish accent, Alby suggested we go outside and get a little fresh air.

As we headed for the door we saw Gus and Sheila, hand in hand, on their way out ahead of us. By now the rain had stopped. The lights from the hall lit up a wide swath of the playground and we saw Gus and Sheila disappear into one of the school's old brick air raid shelters that had been left standing for storage purposes.

'Come on,' said Alby, 'let's have a bit of fun.'

'What do you have in mind?' I asked.

Alby winked. 'You'll see.'

I followed him over to the entrance of the shelter into which Gus and Sheila gone. 'Listen,' he whispered. At first I could hear only muffled voices, but soon there were sounds of heavy breathing and moaning, then Sheila shouting 'Yes, yes, yes.'

'Get ready to run for it,' Alby whispered. 'Quiet now. We'll need to get across to the bike sheds as quick as we can go. You ready?'

I nodded.

Alby leaned his head into the shelter entrance and in as deep and booming a voice as he could muster, called into the darkness, 'This is God. I'm watching you sinners!'

A moment later we were sprinting to the dark side of the playground. As we ducked behind the bicycle sheds, Gus's voice rang out, 'Bleeding peeping tom. If I get my hands on you, I'll…'

We sat choking back giggles for several minutes before we decided it was safe to head back to the party. As we slipped into the hall Gus was at the bar talking to Stan and his best man. Gus spotted us and came over. 'Where've you two been?'

'To get a breath of fresh air,' said Alby.

'You didn't see anybody lurking around, did you?'

'Not a soul,' said Alby. 'Why do you ask?'

'Something that happened out there a few minutes ago.'

Alby put on a concerned expression. 'What was that?'

'You could call it an act of God,' said Gus.

100

'They say he works in mysterious ways,' said Alby.

Gus didn't look amused, but perhaps it was because he had just spotted Sheila dancing cheek to cheek with one of the guests in a gabardine suit. Gus marched over to reclaim her.

I changed my mind about asking Sheila for a dance; somehow I didn't fancy her any more. My disillusion was complete when Alby told me he had noticed there were damp patches under her arms and she ponged a bit.'

My envy of Gus now totally evaporated, and I began to enjoy the party. Alby and me even joined in some of the singing and, after a couple of glasses of stout consumed surreptitiously in the school kitchen, we plucked up enough courage to take to the dance floor. Despite the rudimentary steps Alby had learned from Enid and passed on to me, we subjected our unfortunate partners to an ordeal of toe trampling and collisions with other couples. Perhaps our partners were mellowed by alcohol, but most of them seemed to endure it with remarkable stoicism.

As the evening wore on and we had downed more stout in the kitchen our confidence grew. By the time of the last waltz, in which our partners were two busty machinists from Stan's firm, we had begun to imagine ourselves as a couple of budding Rudolph Valentinos. But when Alby asked if we could escort the girls home, they began tittering. 'We don't want to get arrested for baby snatching,' said the redhead Alby had been dancing with. 'In any case we've got a lift arranged,' said my peroxided partner.

'Didn't really fancy either of them that much,' said Alby as we got our coats from the boys' cloakroom.

'Nor me,' I said, wishing I believed it.

'Anyway I feel pretty knackered,' said Alby.

'You look it,' I said.

It had been arranged that Alby would sleep at my house because at Christmas and New Year and other celebratory occasions, every available bed, armchair and square foot of floor space in the Wilson household was usually occupied by family guests who had missed their last bus or were too drunk to make their way home.

We slept in late the next morning, and Alby woke looking pale and haggard. It could have been a hangover, but he hadn't drunk any more than me and I felt only mildly jaded. Then I remembered winning the race to the wedding reception, and him looking like death warmed up. Though he'd made a joke of it, I knew Alby didn't much like losing at anything.

'How're you feeling?' I asked as we got dressed.

'I'm okay,' he said.

'You sure? You don't look too great.'

He put his arm around my shoulder. 'Stop worrying, mate, I'm indestructible, you should know that.'

For the first time in my life I began to wonder if he was.

102

CHAPTER TEN

After Alby had gone home I couldn't get him out of my mind. I went into the kitchen, where my mother was cooking Sunday lunch, and asked her if she had noticed Alby had been looking under the weather.

'Now you mention it I suppose he hasn't been quite his old self lately,' she said, as she basted a leg of lamb. 'Perhaps he's a bit run-down. Knowing him, I expect he'll be right as rain again soon.'

'I hope you're right,' I said.

The meat hissed and sizzled as my mother spooned fat over it before pushing the pan back in the oven. Then she placed a string-bag of peas and a colander on the table. 'Be a love,' she said, 'and shell these while I do the potatoes.' It was a task she knew I didn't mind because I enjoyed helping myself to the fresh, raw peas as I stripped them from their shells.

For a while my mother stood quietly at the sink peeling the red King Edward potatoes, then, without looking up, she said, 'I thought Enid looked lovely at her wedding.'

'Where did you see her?' I asked.

'I watched her arrive at the church.'

'Funny, I didn't see you.'

'Made myself scarce. I stood in a shop doorway on the other side of the road.   Felt a bit silly standing there on my own with tears trickling down my cheeks.'

'You should have come into the church,' I said.

'You didn't need an official invitation to sit and watch the service.'

'I'd love to have been there,' she said. 'I've known Enid all her life. But your father would probably have been furious if I'd gone to the service.'

'Because of that daft bust-up with Alby's dad?'

My mother nodded. 'Yes, it's very silly, and it's sad.'

'What do you think it would take to get them speaking again?'

'I don't know.' She held up her hands in a gesture of helplessness. 'They're both such obstinate men.'

'But there must be some way.'

'I think Mr Wilson would have to apologise to your father. After all he practically accused him of cowardice.'

The feud had been going on for more than a year. It had begun during a game of dominoes at the Hare and Hounds, but neither my father nor Alby's would talk about it. We did, however, get a version of events from our classmate Eddie Coates, whose dad had also been taking part in the game. Seems it flared up late in the evening after everyone present was well tanked up. Cliff Wilson had been going on about his experiences with the Desert Rats in the Western Desert during the war, repeating stuff they had all heard before, until eventually my father told him to give it a rest and get on with the game. Mr Wilson then apparently accused my father of having had a cushy, well-paid time during the war while his mates were putting their lives on the line. According to Eddie's version, my father got up and walked out of the pub.

Knowing Alby's dad I doubt if he would have said what he did if he had been sober, but he obviously touched a very raw nerve. Thankfully the feud didn't affect my friendship with Alby. In fact my father seemed to go out of his way to be pleasant to Alby whenever he saw him and Mr Wilson was just as friendly to me.

My mother's voice broke into my thoughts. 'Are you going to finish shelling those peas or sit day-dreaming all morning?'

'Sorry, mum, I was miles away.'

She smiled. 'I could see that. What were you thinking about?'

'Dad. How hard did he try to get into the forces during the war?'

'He doesn't like talking about those days,' she said, 'but I do remember him going to the recruiting office, and being turned down because he was in what they classed as a reserved occupation.'

'What did that mean?'

'His factory had switched from making gas meters to turning out parts for tanks. As a toolmaker he was reckoned to be too useful to the war effort to be allowed to go off and join the forces.'

'But if he'd wanted to go badly enough, I'd have though they would let him,' I said.

My mother shrugged. 'I don't know, love. But I think his age may have been   against him as well.'

I did a quick calculation and worked out that he must have been thirty-five when the war began. 'I'm sure a lot of people his age were called up,' I said, 'especially later on in the war after so many men had been killed or wounded.'

'I shouldn't lose any sleep over it,' said my mother. 'What's past is past. And there'd be no good upsetting your father by bringing it up.'

I finished shelling the peas and was about to go and do my French homework when my father came into the kitchen. 'I'm off then,' he said. 'Expect I'll be home the back of two.'

'Dinner will be ready at half past two,' my mother called as he disappeared.

'Bet it'll be more like three o'clock as usual before he gets home,' I said.

My mother didn't answer. We both knew this Sunday would probably be no different to most others. My father and his mates would be drinking in the Hare and Hounds until the two o'clock closing time, after which they would typically continue arguing and joshing outside the pub until they eventually drifted off home, voluble and beery-breathed, to try and placate their wives, and eat a warmed over Sunday dinner. In my father's case this would invariably be followed by a nap and half an hour with the *News of the World*. In the evening he and his pals would meet up once more in the saloon bar of the Hare and Hounds to take up where they had left off earlier.

After my father had gone I went into the living room to finish my homework, but found it difficult to concentrate. Not for the first time I had the uneasy feeling that I was in breach of that commandment about honouring your father. If, as I suspected, many father-son relationships were of the love-hate variety, I felt sure that in most cases, unlike my own, love was the overriding emotion.

I had felt anything but love for my father a couple of nights before when I lay in bed listening to him and my mother having one of their frequent rows. I couldn't hear clearly much of what was said, but there was no mistaking the anger in their voices. My father was the worse for drink and doing most of the shouting. At one point I heard him call my mother a high and mighty bitch, and going on about a married man's rights. There was a crash like the sound of furniture being knocked over, then silence. The silence worried me more than the arguing.

The next morning my mother had a big purple bruise under one eye, which hadn't been there when I said good night to her. It wasn't the first time I'd seen such marks on her, but she never complained in my hearing. In fact, I heard her more than once defend my father when my Gran Wright criticised him over his boozing or gambling habits. My mother would insist he had his good points. She seemed to accept that her lot was what life had marked our for her and that she just had to make the best of it.

I put my French homework on one side and decided to have a quiet chat with the Big Fellah. I'd been getting a little impatient to see some evidence he had been taking notice of the matters I'd recently been bringing to his attention. 'Lord,' I began, dropping the customary 'Dear' to let him know I wasn't feeling too chummy, 'you may have your reasons for allowing my old man to go on treating my mother the way he does, but it doesn't seem at all Christian to me. Give me one good reason why I should honour him like your commandment says I'm supposed to? Just because we share the same name and have the same blood running through our veins, that surely doesn't mean I have to turn a blind eye to everything he gets up to. Other people have to earn our respect, why not fathers?'

On the Sunday evening after tea I decided to go round to Alby's to see if he could offer some words of

107

wisdom in the absence of any action by the Big Fellah. We sat on his bed and played draughts while I unburdened myself. Alby was aware how I felt about my father, but this was the first time I had let on about him laying in to my mother.

Alby said little as he steadily cleared my pieces from the board. Then, after taking my final three draughts in a zig-zag movement with a king, he lay back on the bed. 'Has your mum ever talked about walking out on your old man?'

'Not to me,' I said. 'I don't think she'll go until they carry her out in her coffin.'

'That's the trouble with the womenfolk round here,' said Alby. 'Some of them put up with real nasty buggers because they can't afford to take off. Trouble is most of them wouldn't have anywhere to go and nothing to live on, and their blokes know it.'

'And most of them wouldn't want to leave their kids,' I said.

Alby nodded. 'D'you reckon your mum really hates your old man?'

'I don't think she's capable of hating anyone, but she must come close to it at times. Even so she still seems to find good in him.'

'I suppose everybody's got some good in them,' said Alby. 'Trouble is a lot of folk keep it too bloody well hidden.'

'You can count my old man in with that lot,' I said. 'I just wish my mum had married somebody more like your dad.'

'I love him,' said Alby, 'but even he's not perfect. Nobody is.'

108

'At least he's not a bully, or…' I hesitated.

'Or what?' said Alby.

I didn't answer.

'Were you going to say coward?'

I nodded.

'Not a nice word to hang on your own flesh and blood, even if you haven't got much time for him,' said Alby.

'It seems to be what your dad thinks of him,' I said.

'That was the booze talking,' said Alby. 'They were pretty good mates before.'

'I find it too depressing to talk about,' I said. 'Let's have another game of draughts.'

'I could do with a bit of fresh air,' said Alby. 'Fancy a walk?'

'Where to?'

'How about Potters for a game of snooker?'

'Why not.'

'Got any money?'

I fished out the coins in my pocket. 'Two and threepence left out of my pocket money.'

'And I've got three bob card winnings,' said Alby. 'Plenty for a couple of hours snooker.'

Sunday nights were popular at *Potters' Billiard Hall*. As we walked in it was obvious from the thickness of the pall of cigarette smoke hanging over the long low room that business was brisk. The elderly doorman seated at a desk just inside the entrance looked up with a nod of recognition as we walked in.

'How you doing, young Gil?' Alby inquired.

'Can't grumble, Alb,' said the old man, without removing the half-smoked cigarette from the corner of his mouth. He checked the names on the sheet in front of him. 'All the tables are full and there's two foursomes waiting. I'll give you a shout when there's a table free.'

We sat down on one of the ageing mock leather settees along the side of the hall. Gazing idly around, I became aware of something I hadn't noticed before - the greenness of the place. It wasn't just the baize tables, but the settees, the walls, the ceilings and the linoleum on the floors; even the cigarette smoke seemed to have a greenish tinge. I passed on my observation to Alby.

He grinned. 'Well, England's supposed to be a green and pleasant land.'

When eventually the doorkeeper called out our names, it was to tell us the two players on table nine were into their last five minutes and we were next on. After they had finished they passed their cues to us. 'Good sticks these; straight as dies,' said one. 'More than you can say for the table,' said the other. 'Bleedin' cushes feel like they're padded with cement.'

Alby set up the balls with practised efficiency, and put two shillings in the coin meter to switch on the table lights. He suggested we play for twopence a game.

'Okay,' I said, 'but only if I get two blacks start.'

'Go on then,' said Alby with mock resignation. 'You know me, always a soft touch.'

'That'll be the day,' I said.

We were nearing the end of our third game, with Alby already fourpence to the good, when he muttered, 'Look who's talking to Gil.'

I glanced towards the entrance and was horrified to see Frankie Beckett and Mick Golding in conversation with the doorman.

110

'Take no notice,' said Alby. 'Pretend we haven't seen them.'

On my next turn I attempted to pot a simple red, miscued and sent the white spinning into a middle pocket.

'Think you need three snookers now,' said Alby.

'I surrender,' I said.

'You sure?'

'Seem to have lost my concentration all of a sudden,' I said. 'Don't you think we ought to get going.'

'Yes,' said Alby, 'that might be a good idea.'

I was putting on my jacket when I felt a hand on my shoulder. 'Well well,' said Frankie Beckett, 'if it isn't the little swot. I've been hoping I'd bump into you outside school.'

'Why's that?' I asked, knowing only too well.

Frankie turned to Mick. 'He wants to know why I've been looking for him.'

Mick guffawed and Frankie fixed me with a stare like he was reading my mind. 'Just going were you?'

'Well, yes…'

'Then me and Mick'll come along with you. It's nice and dark outside. We'll take care of you, in a manner of speaking.'

'What about our game of snooker, Frankie?' said Mick.

'It can wait.'

'Tell you what Frankie,' Alby piped up, 'how about you and Mick playing me and Matt? We could have a little side bet as well, if you fancy it.'

'What d'you think Frank?' said Mick. 'Us against them. Easy pickings.'

Frankie turned to Alby and me. 'How much you

two got on you?'

'I've got about two bob,' I said.

Alby said he had a shilling.

'Three bob between you,' said Frankie. 'That'll cover the cost of the table and a bet. We'll play best of three. A bob for the winners. Any objections?'

'Who's going to feed the meter and switch on the lights to start?' I asked.

'Don't ask silly questions,' said Frankie. 'Get on with it.'

'Do we get a refund if we beat you?' asked Alby.

'I just told your mate not to ask silly questions,' said Frankie.

'Hope you'll at least have the decency to pay up on the side bet if we beat you,' said Alby.

Frankie placed a hand under Alby's chin and lifted it slowly. 'One of these days Wilson, I'm going to shove that tongue of yours down your throat so hard it'll come out of your arse.'

'That'd be a tricky place to have to talk out of,' said Alby. 'Mind you, some people seem to manage it.'

'Shut it,' said Frankie, 'and set up the balls.'

Mick tossed a coin for break-off and Alby called correctly. 'We'll start,' he said, chalking his cue. His opening shot left the white ball tight on the baulk cushion.

'Jammy bastard,' muttered Frankie, but he managed to respond with a safety shot which almost snookered me, leaving only a difficult long red. I got a thin connection but left the red over a middle pocket. Mick clipped it in and followed up with a black and another red and blue before leaving the white safe again. In the course of the next few minutes Alby missed several pots of the kind he'd been

112

sinking with ease during our games together, though he never left Frankie an easy opening. I would have been worried if Alby hadn't winked at me on a couple of occasions as his shots went narrowly wide of the target.

'Well played lads,' said Alby after Frankie and Mick had won the first game by a comfortable margin. 'You knocked in some shots Joe Davis would have been pleased with'

'Cut the crap and get on with it,' said Frankie.

The second game looked to be going the same way as the first, but a late break of twenty-seven by Alby enabled us to take it on the pink. 'Had a bit of luck that time,' he said.

Our opponents stayed silent.

'Our turn to start,' said Frankie, breaking off in the third game before we had chance to argue there should be a toss-up for the decider. His opening shot left Alby with a distant red on, which he potted and went on to make a break of nineteen. Mick came back a couple of turns later with a twenty-one, but then the game became tight with no-one reaching double figures again. I managed to contain my nervousness and make the odd pot and avoid foul shots, but it was Alby and Mick who did most of the scoring. The game eventually went to the black and after a long bout of safety play, Mick overhit a shot which left me a fairly easy shot into a corner pocket. As I was about to hit the ball, Frankie leaned forward and whispered into my ear, 'Only a prat could miss that.' It was enough to cause me to miscue. The black spun several inches wide of the target, rolled slowly along the cushion and, with just about its last roll, fell into the opposite corner pocket.

Alby grinned. 'What do you think of that then,

Frankie? Not a bad trick shot by my partner, eh?'

'Biggest fucking fluke I ever saw,' said Frankie.

'Even so, I think it means you lose the bet,'said Alby.

Frankie smirked. 'Wrong. Call it insurance money; save you coming to any harm on your way home.' Then he turned to me. 'See you real soon arse-licker.'

As he and Mick Golding walked off through the haze of cigarette smoke, Alby smiled. 'Useful we'd got used to those hard cushes before we played them. Made it even easier to win.'

'Might have been better if we'd lost,' I said. 'I didn't like the look on Frankie's face when he said he'd see me soon.'

'He's a bad loser,' said Alby. 'The main thing is not to give him the pleasure of seeing you're scared of him, even if he knows you are.'

'I think he's enjoying playing a cat and mouse game,' I said. 'However he intends to take his revenge, I just wish he'd get on with it.'

'Whatever happens,' said Alby, 'remember Wilson's law: The good guys always come out on top in the end.'

As we left the snooker hall and walked out into the shadowy lamp-lit street I half expected to see Frankie and Mick waiting for us, but the street was deserted apart from an elderly man exercising his spaniel.

We walked quickly, keeping a wary eye out for any figures hovering in the shadows. As we reached Sharkey Road we could hear the distant sounds of a party in progress.

'At least while they're having a shindig and beating

the daylights out of each other, they're leaving other people alone,' said Alby.

As we said good night I decided that, while having Alby as a friend didn't make the world a safer place, it somehow made the dangers a little easier to face.

CHAPTER ELEVEN

When Alby called for me on the Monday morning the first thing I noticed was the dark circles under his eyes. He seemed to read my thoughts. 'Okay, I know I look a bit shagged out,' he said.

'What's up?' I asked.

'Didn't sleep much. My guts were giving me gyp. Maybe something I ate.'

'You should have stayed home.'

'Nah, it's not that bad. Anyway I need to get a bet on. Got a couple of stonewall certs at Haydock from Captain Winsome. You can come in on it if you like.'

'No thanks,' I said, 'I lost my dinner money on your last so-called certs from Captain Winsome.'

'That was pure bad luck.'

'Gambling's a mug's game.'

Alby smiled patiently. 'Any millionaire will tell you you've got to speculate to accumulate.'

'They probably didn't speculate on horses to make their money,' I said. 'I wouldn't be surprised if Captain Winsome is a millionaire. Flogging tips to other people is probably a lot more profitable than risking his own cash on bets.'

'Good luck to him,' said Alby. 'Anyway I'm sure we'll both be millionaires some day. You'll probably just take a bit longer than me.'

As we hurried to the bus stop I was conscious of Alby breathing a little more heavily than usual, and I noticed tiny beads of sweat on his forehead and the back of his neck. We had cut it fine as usual, making it to school just before the bell sounded for assembly.

By the time we sat down at our desks for the first lesson of the day, Alby's face had assumed a colour akin to that of our regulation grey flannel trousers.

'You quite sure you're okay?' I asked him.

He tapped his abdomen. 'Just feel a bit fragile down here, that's all.'

Watching him during the English Lit. lesson and later in Biology, I noticed his head nodding forward now and then as if he was about to doze off, but each time he would immediately sit up very straight with his gaze fixed on the teacher. He managed to negotiate the morning lessons without attracting the teacher's attention, though at one point when we were dissecting frog's legs preserved in formaldehyde he looked as if he was about to be sick. 'This stuff they pickle the croakers in smells worse than Uncle Wally's farts,' he whispered.

I wasn't surprised when Alby said he didn't feel like school dinner. So, after paying a visit to the bookie's runner, we bought ourselves a bag of crisps each and a bottle of orangeade from the outdoor at the Green Lion, and spent most of the lunch hour lying in the shade beneath the beech trees in a quiet corner of the school playing field.

The first lesson of the afternoon was History with Dr Theodore Seligman, known to his pupils as 'Sleepy' because of his slow delivery and laid back style of teaching. Sleepy made no secret of the fact that he would be far happier indulging his passion for bird watching than attempting to illuminate the past for a roomful of largely disinterested teenagers. His lessons were generally

117

reckoned to be the easiest in which to escape detection if you felt like a quiet snooze or indulging in a little doodling, especially if you could obscure yourself behind someone of sizeable girth. Alby occupied the desk to my right immediately behind Tubbo Simms, who was by some margin the most corpulent member of the Fourth Form.

On this particular afternoon Dr Seligman was trying to enlighten us about the rise and fall of Maximilien de Robespierre during the French Revolution. As he droned on about the Third Estate and the Committee of Public Safety and the Thermidor period and the Girondins, I noticed Alby had his head cupped in his hands and his eyes were closed. By the time the bell rang to signal the end of the period, Alby was sleeping soundly. I shook his arm and he sat up quickly, blinking but alert.

As we headed out of the classroom for our next lesson, Dr Seligman called Alby over and asked, 'Are you all right, Wilson?'

'Er… yes sir,' said Alby.

'You most certainly don't look it.'

'It's nothing serious, sir.'

'Hmm, I hope not,' said Sleepy. 'I hadn't the heart to wake you during the lesson.'

Alby flushed. 'Sorry sir, I've been a bit under the weather.'

'Have you seen a doctor?'

'No, sir.'

'You should.'

'I will, sir.'

As we walked out into the playground Alby shook his head. 'Old Sleepy's not as half-soaked as he seems.'

'Did you mean it when you said you'd see the

118

doctor?' I asked.

'Might do. I'll see how it goes.'

'Do you want me to make you a copy of the notes I took in Sleepy's lesson?'

'No need, I've read loads of stuff about the French Revolution. One of my favourite bits of history. Much more interesting books about it in the Thornfield Library than in the school textbooks.'

The final session of the afternoon was a double lesson of Chemistry. It was a subject which happened to be one Alby enjoyed and he was able to remain awake during the lecture and the laboratory session which followed.

When we headed out of the lab at the end of the afternoon, Alby told me he'd be opting out of his paper round. 'Give Lucy my love,' he said. 'Tell her I'm sorry to ruin her day by depriving her of my presence.'

I watched him climb wearily aboard the 44 bus, then I set off along Stackley Road for Spicers' Newsagents.

When I passed on Alby's message to Lucy she shook her head smiling. 'He's a cheeky young blighter, but I'm really sorry he's not well. Do give him my best.'

'I will,' I said

Lucy leaned forward as if about to share a secret. 'Could you do us a big favour, Matt?'

I felt a quiver of anticipation. 'What's that?'

'Do you think you could possibly manage Alby's round as well as your own tonight? We'll be really stuck otherwise.'

'I would but…'

'What is it, Matty?' Lucy had never called me Matty before, and I liked the feeling of a new intimacy between us.

119

'I've got quite a load of homework tonight,' I fibbed, 'but okay, just for you I'll take Alby's papers.'

'Thanks, you're a real pet,' said Lucy. The idea of being her pet seemed distinctly appealing.

'You and Alby are really good mates aren't you?' she said as she counted out the extra evening papers for my bag.

'The best,' I said.

'I can understand why you're so fond of him,' she said.

As I left the shop, Lucy called, 'Don't forget to give Alby my love.'

'I won't,' |I called, and blew her a kiss the way Alby often did.

CHAPTER TWELVE

Alby didn't show up for school the next day, and after my evening meal I went round to his house. His mother said he was in bed, but she greeted me warmly and invited me in.

'He's spent most of the day sleeping,' she said. 'It's not like Alby, he's usually so full of beans.'

'Has the doctor been?' I asked.

'He's coming round this evening after surgery,' said Mrs Wilson.

'What do you think it is?'

'Wouldn't surprise me if it's something he's caught swimming in the canal.'

I told her we hadn't been near the canal since the day we found Hetty Peck's body.

At that moment the door to the stairs opened and Alby appeared. The pallor of his face seemed to highlight the freckles on his cheeks and forehead. 'I thought I heard young Matthew's voice,' he said.

'What are you doing out of bed?' said Mrs Wilson, plainly more concerned than cross.

'Just being sociable,' said Alby. 'Have to make guests feel welcome.' He sat down in an armchair in front of the fire. Simulating the panting of a thirsty dog, he said, 'I could drink a couple of wells dry.'

'I'll get you some lemon squash,' said Mrs Wilson.

'Could you make that plain cold water please, mum,' said Alby.

'Whatever you like, love,' she said, heading into the

kitchen.

Alby winked at me. 'What a nursemaid eh?'

'Do you feel as lousy as you look?' I asked.

'Like a piece of chewed string,' he said. 'I've decided to let the quack take a look.'

Mrs Wilson came back into the room and handed Alby a glass of water.

'Cheers,' he said, taking a long gulp. Then he turned to me. 'Fancy a game of Monopoly?'

'Can't,' I said. 'Have to get back and do my homework.'

'What have you got?'

'Physics and French.'

'You should have brought it round. I could have given you a hand.'

'Thanks,' I said, 'but I reckon you ought to be taking it easy for a bit.'

Later, as I got up to leave, Alby said, 'Might see you tomorrow then, if the quack says I'm okay to go to school.'

'I don't think you'll be going anywhere tomorrow,' said Mrs Wilson.

'We'll see,' said Alby.

Mrs Wilson was wrong. Alby did go somewhere the next day, but it wasn't to school, it was to the General Hospital.

'It all happened so quickly,' said Mrs Wilson, when I called round in the evening. 'Our doctor examined Alby and sent for an ambulance straight away.'

'Did the doctor say what was wrong? I asked.

''No, said he couldn't be sure, and that the hospital would have to do tests to find out exactly what it was.'

The hospital kept Alby in until the weekend, and visiting was restricted to his family. When I turned up at his house on the Saturday afternoon he was sitting in front of the fire reading *John Bull* magazine.

'Glad you came round mate,' he said. 'I could do with a chinwag.' He looked me up and down. 'You still seem to be in one piece. I've been worried Frankie might have made his move when I wasn't around to look after you.'

'Maybe he's thought better of it,' I said, more in hope than conviction. 'Anyway, I haven't come to talk about Frankie Beckett. How are you feeling?'

Alby shrugged. 'Bit like I've just run up and down Ben Nevis and then done fifteen rounds with Joe Louis. Apart from that no problem at all.'

'What happened in the hospital?' I asked.

'Lot of fun and games,' he said. 'After the x-ray folk had finished filming my innards from all angles the boss quack and his sidekicks took turns seeing how deep they could poke their fingers into my guts, then another joker came along with a syringe and sucked enough blood out of me to keep Dracula in party mood for a month. But they saved the best 'til last. They put me to sleep, then slit me open and took out a piece of the lump they'd discovered in here.' He pointed at a spot just below his ribs.

'Is it sore?'

'Bit tender, yes.'

'Expect they had to do all that stuff to find out exactly what's wrong with you.'

'I wouldn't mind if they weren't so bloody cheerful while they're doing it,' said Alby. 'Never mind, there was a cracking little blonde nurse on the night shift. Got her to hold my hand a couple of times.'

'What did you find out?'

'She wouldn't give me her telephone number.'

'I mean did the doctors tell you what their tests turned up?'

'They did some more tests yesterday. Haven't got all the results yet. Mum and me have to go back to the hospital Tuesday to get a run-down from the head quack.'

I could hardly wait to get round to Alby's house on the Tuesday evening to find out what the specialist had reported. When I arrived Alby was sitting at the dining table playing Patience. 'Daft game,' he said, 'I always win in the end. Just bend the rules a bit until I turn up the cards I need.' He sank down on the sofa in front of the fire and gestured for me to join him. Sniffing the air, his face lit up. A fruity aroma was drifting in from the kitchen. 'Mmm, my favourite smell in the world. Mum's baking one of her specials.'

I knew he meant a Dundee cake. Bulging with fruit and covered with a shiny crust of almonds, Mrs Wilson's cakes were renowned among Alby's friends. Sometimes when we played games at his house his mother would supply us with slices of the cake along with cups of tea or lemonade.

'She's making it for me to take into hospital,' said Alby. 'Can't stomach too much of the hospital grub.'

'When do you have to go back in?' I asked.

'Tomorrow.'

'What did the specialist tell you?'

'The lump they found is a pretty big one,' he said. 'It's what they call a malignant tumour.'

124

I said it sounded nasty and wondered if it hurt.

'Not when I'm sitting up straight,' said Alby. 'Bit uncomfortable when I lie on my side. I think the lump presses against the other organs in my guts.'

'Can you feel the lump from the outside?'

Alby nodded. 'If you push your fingers into the right place. I'd let you have a poke like the quacks have been doing, but it's a bit too tender.'

'How big is it?'

'Heard one of the junior docs telling a nurse it was the size of a hand grenade.'

'Like a pineapple?'

'I suppose so. I don't think he meant one of those jerry hand grenades with the long handles.'

'Wonder what caused it?'

Alby assumed a mock grimace. 'Maybe too many school dinners.'

'Remember when you got hit in the stomach by that ball from Mick Golding in the nets last year?' I said. 'I wonder if that could have set it off?'

'Trouble is nobody knows what causes the bloody things,' said Alby. 'Maybe I'll have to become a scientist and sort it all out.'

'What happens next?'

'The boss quack said it's too risky to try cutting it out. The lump's in a really tricky spot right up against the aorta.'

'The what?'

'The big artery that comes out of your ticker.'

'Must be something they can do.'

'Oh yes,' said Alby, 'it consists mainly of blasting the lump with radiation.'

'Don't like the sound of that much,' I said.

Mrs Wilson came in with two mugs of tea and a plate of chocolate biscuits. 'Have you told Matt about Cornwall?' she asked Alby.

'Haven't got around to it yet,' he said, 'we've been too busy gassing about you know what.'

After Mrs Wilson had returned to the kitchen I asked Alby what he was supposed to tell me about Cornwall.

'Fancy a week's holiday down there?' he said.

'Daft question,' I said. 'Of course I do.'

'My dad's been offered the use of a flat for a week,' said Alby. 'It's owned by his gaffer. He came up with the offer after he heard about my little problem.'

'When are you going?' I asked.

'Couple of weeks time,' said Alby. 'After school breaks up for the summer hols.'

'But mightn't you be in hospital?'

'The quacks say I'll have finished my first lot of radiation treatment by then, and they reckon a break by the seaside would do me good. Dad's arranged to borrow my Uncle Bill's car for the trip. The week won't cost you anything apart from a bit of spending money.'

'Which part of Cornwall are you going to?' I asked.

'Place called Polzeath,' said Alby. 'Nobody's ever heard of it, but it's supposed to have brilliant surf. And the flat's in spitting distance of the beach. Do you think your old man will let you come?'

Hope he won't be awkward about it,' I said. 'He didn't stop me going to Enid's wedding,'

I'd only been to the seaside once before, on a charabanc outing to Blackpool with the Hare and Hounds

126

Darts Club in the summer of 1946. Alby and me had been among a handful of members' children allowed to go along to fill up spare seats on the coach.

When I reminded Alby of the trip, he looked rueful. 'What a day,' he said, 'a coach-load of hardened boozers out for a good time and a bunch of kids moaning most of the day because they were fed up.'

'At least we got to play on the beach for a bit,' I said.

'Yes,' said Alby, 'but we never got a sniff of the funfair. Spent most of the time hanging about outside pubs getting fobbed off with bags of crisps and glasses of pop while our dads got tanked up.'

'I suppose they were still celebrating the end of the war,' I said.

'Come to think of it, we did learn a few good boozing songs,' said Alby. He began singing the chorus of *Beer Beer, Glorious Beer* before moving seamlessly into the refrain of *I Wish I Was Single Again.*

'Come on Caruso,' I said, 'I'll give you a game of Monopoly. Just a friendly though; I'm broke.'

'Got to have a little bet to make it interesting,' said Alby. 'Tell you what, the loser has to make our beds for the week in Cornwall. That's if your dad lets you go.'

'Okay,' I said, resigning myself to a week's bed making.

CHAPTER THIRTEEN

To my relief my father's reaction to the Wilsons' invitation to accompany them to Cornwall was one of scarcely concealed indifference. My mother was predictably delighted since the customary parlous state of the family's finances meant that the nearest we ever got to going on holiday was spending a few days at my Great Aunt Beryl's in Shrewsbury.

It was arranged that the Wilsons would call for me at six o'clock on the Saturday morning. At the appointed time there was a sharp rap on the knocker and I opened the door to find Alby standing there. 'Your limousine awaits, sir,' he announced, bowing deeply.

'Thank you my good fellow,' I said. 'I'll be with you in a trice.' I grabbed my small suitcase and kissed my mother, who had woken me early and ensured I had a hot drink and a bowl of porridge 'to set me up for the journey'. As I followed Alby up the path, she called, 'Be careful in the sea. Don't get out of your depth.' I hoped Alby wasn't listening.

Mr Wilson manoeuvred my small suitcase into the already tightly packed boot of Uncle Bill's elderly but lovingly maintained Jowett saloon, and I climbed into the back seat beside Alby. The Jowett reeked of old leather and tobacco, and the space was cramped for someone with legs as long as mine, but I felt like royalty. This beat a corporation bus any day.

'Sounds like an old lawn mower,' said Alby as the

Jowett chugged through the suburbs and out into the Warwickshire countryside.

'She's no Roller, but she's a good old trouper,' said Mr Wilson. 'If you treat her with proper respect she'd take you to Timbuktoo and back, no trouble at all. Run up the side of a house in second gear.'

'Just as long as it gets us to Polzeath and home again,' said Mrs Wilson, the top of her freshly permed hair just visible above the front passenger seat.

'Don't worry, my love,' her husband assured her. 'Bill's had her for ten years, and she's never let him down. A real gem, just like you.'

Mrs Wilson laughed and passed round a bag of pear drops.

With not much to look at out of the car windows apart from hedges and fields and the occasional huddle of cottages, Alby and me started playing *I Spy*, then *Animal, Vegetable and Mineral.* He caught me out a few times with his knowledge of historical figures and scientific terms before I tripped him up with the name of a fairly obscure Essex cricketer whose name I'd happened to notice on the sports pages of the *Evening Mail* the day before after he'd scored a double century in a county match. After that we began challenging each other with tongue twisters. We both managed to keep going for quite a while with rapid repetitions of the familiar *Peter Piper Picked a Peck of Pickled Peppers,* but then Alby thought up a new one, *Scrawny Shawnee Squaw,* with which he easily outlasted me. We got bored with that game though, and Alby produced his pocket chess set. By the time we reached Cirencester, he had already checkmated me and was about to do it again as we approached Bath.

As we headed deeper into Somerset the afternoon sun grew hotter and the car became stuffier. Alby dozed off and I was beginning to feel drowsy myself when I heard Mrs Wilson say, 'Don't you think we ought to stop for a break soon, Cliff?'

'Of course, my sweet,' he replied. 'Just as soon as we spot a nice pub.'

A few minutes later we were pulling into the car park of what turned out to be a pleasant little hostelry called the Swan and Bucket. The Jowett gave a shudder as Mr Wilson turned off the ignition, and Alby woke up. 'I could murder a glass of cider,' he announced when he saw where we were.

We sat at one of the wooden tables in the pub garden and Mr Wilson went off to get sandwiches and drinks. The ham and tomato sandwiches he brought back were freshly made and you could taste the rich salty farm butter. When Alby and me had eaten as much as we wanted and washed it down with sweet cider, he suggested we went for a look around while his folks finished their meal.

'Don't be long,' said Mr Wilson as we strolled off, 'we've still got quite a way to go.'

There was a small gate in the hedge bordering the pub garden so we pushed it open and went through into the adjoining field where a cricket match in progress. With nothing more interesting to look at we stood and watched. Close by a fat, ruddy-faced man was fielding at fine leg. There was a shout of 'Howzat' and a batsman was given lbw. On the other side of the field a man adjusted the scoreboard to read: *Visitors 68 for 9. Home Team 76 all out.*

As the visitors' last batsman, a gangly youth of

130

about sixteen, walked out to the wicket, the shadow of the fat man fell across us. 'Artnoon lads,' he said, wiping sweat from his forehead with the back of his hand. 'Could one of you do me a favour and field for me while I go for a piddle.'

'Is that allowed?' I asked, without thinking.

'We're not fussy round these parts, sonny,' said the fat man. 'It's only village cricket, not a bloody test match.'

'Go on then,' said Alby, 'I'll sub for you.'

'Good lad,' said the fat man, and hurried off into a small clump of trees. As he did so, the new batsman took his stance and the home team bowler, a slow left armer, trundled up and landed the ball on a tuft of grass a yard wide of the stumps. The ball rolled a few inches and stopped dead, at which point the gangly youth stepped across and swung his bat at it, sending the ball skidding along the bumpy turf to the fielder at long-off. He fumbled the ball before hurling it to the wicketkeeper by which time the batsmen had scrambled a single.

Now a man built like Desperate Dan faced the bowling. The hapless bowler sent down a slow full toss, which was promptly despatched to the far corner of the ground where it landed on the corrugated metal roof of the groundsman's hut with a crash that might have been heard in the next county. The six left the visitors' needing just one run to draw level with their hosts and two to win. The bowler muttered some expletive, then trotted in again, sending down a short ball that hit a bare patch of ground and bounced to head height. Desperate Dan swivelled to play a hook, but the ball caught the top edge of his bat and it soared towards deep fine leg where Alby was standing. At that moment the fat man was emerging from the trees, buttoning his flies, and Alby had turned to leave the pitch.

'The ball, Alby,' I shouted, but before I could add 'behind you' he had spun around and put up his hands as if to protect himself. A moment later the rest of the fielders and the smattering of spectators were applauding. The ball had dropped like a mortar shell out of the bright sunlight into Alby's outstretched hands and stuck there as if his palms were coated with glue. I could have sworn he had his eyes closed.

'Bloody amazing,' exclaimed the fat man, clapping Alby on the back. 'Never seen a catch like it. You've won us the game.'

'Always glad to be of service,' said Alby with a wink in my direction.

'You and your chum like to come and have a drink with the team?' asked the fat man.

'Sorry, we can't stop,' said Alby, 'our limousine is waiting. Maybe we'll pop in next time we're passing.'

'Any time,' said the fat man.

'You jammy so and so,' I said, as we headed back to the Swan and Bucket. 'You didn't know much about that catch.'

Alby grinned. 'Saw it coming all the way.'

The Wilsons had finished their lunch and were sitting waiting at the table as we returned to the pub garden. 'Where have you been?' Mrs Wilson wanted to know. 'We were beginning to think you'd got lost.'

'Sorry mum,' said Alby, 'I've just been winning a cricket match.'

His mother nodded patiently. She was used to Alby's little jokes.

It was just leaving two o'clock when we drove

down the steep, curving hill into Polzeath. Mr Wilson stopped the car outside the post office-cum-general store to ask directions to our holiday flat. Through the open windows we could smell the ozone and hear the shriek of seagulls and the shouts of kids playing on the beach.

The flat that was to be our home for the next seven days turned out to be on the top floor of a rambling Edwardian terraced house on the esplanade which ran along the top of the cliffs above the beach. The main room was long and narrow with a large panoramic window, spattered on the outside with salt flecks, and offering a magnificent view across the bay. The white distempered walls and ceilings were mottled with brown damp spots, and old prints of sailing ships and seascapes hung in uneven groupings. The furnishings consisted mainly of old armchairs, a pull-out sofa bed along one wall and a dining table surrounded by four wooden folding chairs. Beside a big stone fireplace, there was an oak bookcase filled with old books, their spines faded by the sunlight.

Alby and me were to share a Spartan little room along a narrow corridor at the back of the house. Apart from two single iron frame beds, the only furniture was a small chest of drawers, and a wicker bedroom chair. The room had an oddly reassuring smell of mothballs, reminiscent of my Gran Sheridan's house. We agreed that of all the places we would choose to spend a week, this beat Buckingham Palace and, as far as I was concerned, came a close second to Helen O'Donnell's house.

After we had decided who would sleep in which bed, and emptied the contents of our suitcases into the chest of drawers, we went back to the large sitting room where Mr Wilson was pulling out the sofa bed. He lay on it and bounced up and down. 'Bit hard, but it'll do,' he said.

Mrs Wilson appeared from the kitchenette carrying a tray with four mugs of tea. She put them down on the table and beamed. 'Think you're going to like it here, boys?'

'Got a funny feeling we are,' said Alby.

After we had finished the tea, Alby and me decided to go for a stroll.

'Be careful along the cliff,' said Mrs Wilson, 'It looks really steep.'

'Don't worry, mum,' said Alby, 'I won't let Matt lead me astray.'

As we were leaving, Mrs Wilson said, 'I noticed there was a fish and chip shop in the village. Everybody happy to settle for a meal from there tonight?'

'Great idea,' said Alby, 'and we could eat them out of the wrapping to save washing up.'

Alby's dad and me indicated our enthusiastic support, and Mrs Wilson said, 'That's settled then.'

For the first time since I found out about the nature of Alby's illness, I felt something close to contentment as we strolled along the esplanade together in the late afternoon sunshine. We found a narrow path winding down to the beach and, as we descended , Alby began singing:

I do like to be beside the seaside!
I do like to be beside the sea!
I do like to stroll along the prom prom prom,
With my old mate Matt tiddlyompompom!

As we reached the bottom of the path and stepped onto the sand, he said, 'Get a load of that.'

'What?' I asked, half expecting him to point out some curvaceous girl stretched out sunning herself.

134

'Everything you can see in front of you,' he said.

Across the bay, dark jagged rocks stood guard over the beach and on the green hillside beyond little white-washed houses looking like nature intended them to be part of the landscape. High above, the sun hovered in the cloudless sky like a big yellow beach ball and cast its brightness in diamonds across the inrushing Atlantic rollers. Bellyboarders stood waist deep waiting for the breakers to carry them into the shore. Further out beyond the headland we could see the bobbing heads of more adventurous swimmers.

We stopped and took off our shoes and socks and walked slowly across the sand, enjoying the warmth on the soles of our feet. Around us children played tag and beach cricket while the grown-ups nestled down behind their multi-coloured canvas windbreaks, dozing or reading, or willing the sun to transform their pallid bodies with instant tans.

As we got closer to the water's edge we saw two young lovers scrawling some words in the wet sand with their fingers, then stroll on, leaving their message to the mercy of the incoming tide. Further along the beach a gaggle of old ladies in sensible sweaters and cardigans were chattering happily as they made their way back to the charabanc that had brought them on their outing to the seaside.

'Wonder what it feels like to be old?' said Alby. 'Really old I mean, like some of those ladies getting on the coach.'

'Not something I've thought a lot about,' I said.

'Imagine all the stuff you'd have seen and done,' said Alby. 'Gran Ryder can tell you about things she saw

135

with her own eyes in another century.'

'What sort of things?'

'Her dad going off to the Boer War in his red coat, toffs being driven around in carriages pulled by horses, and thatched cottages and sheep mooching around in fields where factories are now. Must be nice to have all those kind of things to run through your mind when you're lying in bed bored or queuing up for the pictures.'

'Suppose so,' I said, 'but d'you reckon it's worth getting old just so you can have nice memories?'

'Better to grow old than not,' said Alby. 'And before we get any older, let's go and get our fish and chips. And have the best holiday in the history of civilisation.'

CHAPTER FOURTEEN

Shirley and Beth sailed into our lives aboard the ferry boat that plied across the Camel River estuary between Rock and Padstow.

We had been wandering along the beach just beyond Rock village watching the armada of sailing boats on the estuary twisting and turning in the breeze, when we spotted the ferry approaching from Padstow. As it chugged to the water's edge, the ferryman's mate jumped down onto the sand and secured a gangplank against the side of the boat. It was Sunday afternoon and there was only a handful of passengers aboard. Last off were two girls who looked about the same age as Alby and myself. The ferryman said something to them as they came down the gangplank and they giggled.

'Take a look at that chassis,' said Alby eyeing the first of the girls to step onto the sand. She was wearing a white singlet and yellow shorts.

'The one behind her isn't bad either,' I said. She was dressed similarly to the first girl, except that her shorts were blue.

'Come on,' said Alby, 'let's go and see how the land lies.'

We caught up with the girls on the path behind the beach. 'Hi!' said Alby.'Saw you getting off the ferry. Enjoy yourself in Padstow?'

'Yes, thank you,' said the one in yellow shorts. Her

acccnt was what anyone from our estate would have rated seriously posh.

'We were thinking of going across,' said Alby.

'The ferry's still there,' said the girl in blue shorts. 'You could get on if you're quick.'

'We'll probably go tomorrow when the shops are open,' said Alby.

The girls walked on with Alby and me a few paces behind. As they reached the spot where the path joined the road into the village, they stopped, A muddy puddle left by the early morning rain stretched across the width of the path in front of them. Before they could move off the path to go round it, Alby stepped quickly forward, pulled off his windjammer and laid it across the puddle. The girls looked astonished, then began to titter as he took the hand of each in turn and led them across to the dry road surface.

'You didn't need to do that,' said the girl in the yellow shorts. 'You've made an awful mess of your jacket.'

'Tis nothing, dear lady,' said Alby with a bow. 'It is an honour to be of service.'

The girl laughed. 'I should be careful. Sir Walter Raleigh did that and ended up losing his head.'

'I'll take my chances,' said Alby. 'By the way, my name's Albert, known to my wide circle of friends as Alby.' Nodding in my direction, he added, 'This is my associate and confidant, Matthew.'

The girls exchanged grins. When they introduced themselves as Shirley and Beth we were surprised to learn they were twins; neither their physical appearance nor their personalities were alike in any obvious way. We discovered they were a year older than us, so felt obliged to tell a small porky about our age.

138

As we walked up through Rock village Alby continued to do most of the talking and Shirley, the girl in the yellow shorts, most of the responding. Beth and me chipped in now and again, but she seemed happy, as I was, to let the other two chatter on. Although we said little to each other, I thought I sensed something of a rapport developing between Beth and myself, perhaps because we both lacked the easy confidence of the other two.

'We would deem it a rare privilege to see you again,' said Alby as we turned up the steep lane to the cottage where the twins told us they were staying with an elderly aunt.

'You sound like a character from a Jane Austen novel,' said Shirley.

'I can switch to Rudyard Kipling if your prefer,' said Alby. 'I do a great Gunga Din.'

'Are you ever serious?' asked Beth.

'Only when there's an R in the month,' said Alby.

'Try now,' said Shirley.

'Okay,' said Alby, assuming a mock frown. 'Would you and Beth like to meet Matt and me again, say tomorrow?'

'What do you think, Beth?' said Shirley.

I noticed Beth glance momentarily in my direction. 'I don't mind,' she said.

'How about ten o'clock on Rock Beach?' said Alby.

'Make it eleven,' said Shirley.

'Until tomorrow then,' said Alby.

As we walked back through the village, Alby said, 'You were a bit quiet, even for you.'

'I could hardly get a word in edgeways when you started your Prince Charming routine,' I said.

139

'Sorry,' said Alby. 'Suppose I do get a bit carried away at times.'

As we crossed the beach and began walking up the incline to the cliff path, Alby's breathing got progressively more laboured, until eventually it was coming in short rasps.

'Want to stop for a rest?' I said.

'This mountaineering lark is a bit knackering,' said Alby. 'I wouldn't mind a breather.'

After we had lain in the coarse dune grass for a while, Alby sat up and stretched his arms. 'That's better. Got a bit of puff back. You know what, I think we could be on a winner with those twins. I reckon they're game for a bit of fun.'

'Doubt if they'd be interested in the kind of fun I think you've got in mind,' I said. 'Especially Beth.'

'Don't be so sure,' said Alby. 'It's often the quiet ones that are the best sports. Take a look into those dark eyes of hers. I reckon she could have a bit of the gypsy in her.'

'You're beginning to sound like Dipper Dickson,' I said.

Alby chuckled. 'Don't you sometimes wonder if old Dipper's really as big an expert on the seduction of ladies as he makes out?'

'He usually seems to know what he's talking about,' I said.

'I wouldn't deny he's well read on the subject,' said Alby, 'but just because you've read books on how to fly aeroplanes, it doesn't mean you could take one up and start doing aerobatics.'

'I suppose not,' I said.

140

'Do you fancy Beth?' Alby asked.

'Might do,' I said.

'You don't sound too sure,' said Alby. 'Can I have a guess why?'

'Go ahead.'

'Helen O'Donnell. You can't get her out of your mind, can you?'

'Doesn't stop me fancying other girls.'

'Relieved to hear it,' said Alby. 'A bit of fun would do us both good.'

'You may be right there,' I said, 'and anyway, whatever happens wouldn't change the way I feel about Helen.'

Alby shook his head, smiling. 'You've really got her up on a pedestal, haven't you?'

'So what if I have?'

'Amazing really.'

'What is?'

'Your devotion to a girl you've never even got as far as kissing.'

I was tempted to tell him about the kiss Helen had given me when I walked her home, but instead I said, 'I'm sure it's possible to love somebody without all the physical stuff.'

Alby stood up. 'I suppose so. They reckon some blokes fall in love with the painting of the Mona Lisa in that art gallery in Paris.'

'How can you fall in love with some paint on a sheet of canvas?' I said, as we started walking.

'That's folk for you,' said Alby. 'No accounting for what they find to love. Look at my Auntie Bessie with her cats. Got three of them, and talks to them like they're pcople. "What would you like for supper, Tabitha? Think it's going to rain today, Percy? Do you think mummy looks nice in her new dress, Theo?"

'She hasn't got any kids,' I said. 'Maybe cats are the next best thing for her.'

'Suppose everybody needs something to love,' said Alby. 'Look at poofs fancying other blokes. Did you know Guy Barnard, our esteemed sports master, is shacked up with a police sergeant?'

'I don't believe it,' I said. 'Can't think of anybody less like a pansy than him.'

'You can't go by appearances,' said Alby. 'They reckon sailors and convicts are at it all the time.'

'Who told you about Guy Barnard?'

'Dipper Dickson. One of his uncles is a special constable at the Stackfield Road nick.'

'You're putting me off my dinner,' I said.

'They reckon they can't help themselves,' said Alby. 'Born like it. I mean, you couldn't imagine anybody choosing to be that way, not with all the luscious dames there are around.'

'Women sometimes fancy each other as well,' I said.

'Yes I know,' said Alby. 'Terrible waste, isn't it. But I'll tell you one thing, there's no danger of Beth and Shirley being like that. No danger at all.'

That night Alby and me lay nattering well into the small hours about girls and life and death and how good fish and chips taste when you are at the seaside. We slept in late and were glad we hadn't arranged to meet the twins any earlier than eleven o'clock. As it was they turned up half an hour late.

'You're looking exceptionally lovely this morning,' said Alby as they came up to us on Rock Beach. Both were wearing sleeveless cotton summer dresses and sandals.

'What would you like to do on this beautiful morning?' Alby asked.

Shirley smiled. 'Any suggestions?'

'How about a nice walk?' said Alby.

The twins looked at each other, then, as if some kind of telepathy had passed between them, Shirley said 'Okay. Where shall we walk?'

'You knw the lie of the land better than Matt and me,' said Alby, 'so why don't you take us on a mystery tour?'

The girls agreed to lead the way and we set off up the beach and along a path behind the dunes. Soon we came upon the prettiest golf course I had ever seen. Admittedly my previous knowledge of such places had been confined to municipal courses back home where we sometimes trespassed in search of golf balls, which we would sell to the golfers who had lost them in the first place.

This, we learned, was St Enodoc golf course, one of Cornwall's finest, whose immaculately groomed fairways had, according to Shirley, been graced by such worthies as the Prince of Wales, though she wasn't sure which one. As we strolled along a public footpath which ran beside one of the par fives, Alby said, 'I bet it costs a king's ransom to play here.'

'Don't know about that,' said Beth. 'Daddy plays whenever he comes down on holiday.'

'What does your father do for a living?' I asked.

'He's a doctor,' said Beth. 'A GP.'

'Ah,' said Alby. 'Medicine is a vocation I once

considered myself. But I came to realise my talents might be better suited to another calling.'

Shirley wanted to know which calling.

'Haven't finally decided yet,' said Alby, 'but film acting is quite high on my list at the moment.'

Shirley laughed. 'Do you see yourself as a Charlie Chaplin or a Clark Gable?'

'No, I'm more the Leslie Howard type,' said Alby. 'You know, the quintessential English gentleman.'

Both girls giggled. I was used to Alby coming out with unexpected words like quintessential, but to others I suppose it must have sounded a little odd from a kid with his kind of accent. Once when I asked him where he picked up his fancy vocabulary, he said it was mainly from listening to the BBC Home Service and reading the articles in magazines like *John Bull,* and he also read dictionaries for fun.

'Look at that,' said Alby, pointing to a little church that had come into view on the golf course. 'Is it somewhere golfers go to pray for help when they're having a bad round?'

'It's St Enodoc's,' said Beth. 'My favourite church.'

'Not much bigger than our shed,' I said with a modicum of exaggeration.

'That's why we love it,' said Shirley, 'because it's so dinky. Come on, let's go in.'

As we pushed open the heavy wooden door and stepped inside, a sweet, musty smell greeted us. No-one spoke as we made our way to the front of the church; the only sound was the scuff of our feet on the age-polished flagstones. We stood for a few moments in front of the altar, then turned and sat down in the front pew. The girls bowed their heads briefly and I saw Alby close his eyes and mouth some silent words. For a moment his pale face look pensive, then he was smiling again.

'Come on you lot,' he said, getting up, 'churches are for sitting around in on Sundays. It's Monday today.' While Alby had a lot of time for the Big Fellah, I don't think religion was the thing uppermost in his mind on this particular summer morning.

As we resumed our stroll, the golf course seemed almost deserted with just an occasional couple or foursome wending their way along the fairways. Maybe the members were put off by the forecast of showers for the afternoon, which we had
heard on the wireless before we left the flat. While some ominous clouds were massing out at sea, things were beginning to seem quite promising at ground level as we came to the perimeter of the golf course and headed along a path with a signpost pointing to *Daymer Bay*. I noticed Alby had taken Shirley's hand without any apparent objection so I followed suit with Beth.

By the time we reached the dunes around Daymer Bay I had plucked up enough courage to try a tentative kiss and been surprised by the lack of any resistence. I tried again and this time Beth's lips parted slightly. Ahead of us I could see Alby and Shirley lying on a grassy bank behind the dunes. He was on his back with Shirley kissing him like she was serious about it.

I found a sheltered spot between two hummocks a little further along the beach. More kisses and soon buttons were being nervously undone and bra clips fumbled with, and it began to dawn on me that this quiet, well-spoken doctor's daughter was rather more experienced in the ways

145

of the flesh than I was. It was the first time I had kissed a girl with her lips apart and I was startled to feel her tongue darting around inside my mouth like a bee searching for pollen. I grew a little bolder with my fumblings and exposed one of her firm little breasts. I was about to uncover the other when I became aware of spots of rain splashing onto her soft flesh and trickling across the chocolate coloured nipple down towards her armpit.

The heavy grey clouds which now obscured the sun suddenly began unleashing their contents with abandon. Beth giggled and rapidly began buttoning her dress. We ran to a small wooden shelter by the beach car park. A few people were already huddled inside and we were soon joined by Alby and Shirley.

After a while the rain eased to a gentle drizzle, and Shirley said she thought it was time to head home and change into some dry clothes. The pang of frustration I felt was tinged with relief. Although I might possibly have missed a golden opportunity to fulfil one of life's more significant rites of passage, I consoled myself with the thought that if rain hadn't stopped play I would probably have ended up with at best a guilty conscience and at worst maybe even getting a nice girl into trouble.

Perhaps because we were dripping wet, everyone seemed a little subdued as we tramped back through Rock village to the girls' cottage. It was when we asked if we could meet them again that they told us they were leaving for home the next day.

'Daddy's coming to fetch us tomorrow,' said Shirley. 'What a shame we didn't meet sooner.'

'A great pity,' I said.

'Must it all end here?' said Alby, clutching his

146

breast with mock Olivieresque passion.

The twins exchanged glances, and Shirley said, 'We could swop addresses, but I don't think there's much point. People do that on holiday and never get round to writing.'

'Yes,' said Alby. 'Matt and me have never been a great letter writers.' He glanced at me and winked. 'Poetry, prose, definitely, but not dreary old letters.'

'I wouldn't have thought of you as a poet,' said Shirley.

'Just for that I shall write you sonnet,' said Alby.

Shirley laughed. 'What a romantic idea.'

'I can feel it burning in here right now,' said Alby, patting his chest. 'I shall hasten back to our humble lodgings and write while the inspiration is running white hot. Perhaps sometimes on long winter evenings you will look at it and recall the happy moments we spent together. But alas, how shall I be able to send you my immortal words if I don't have your address?'

'Wait a minute,' said Shirley, and hurried up the path to the cottage. Moments later she returned with a card and handed it to Alby. 'Here, have one of daddy's calling cards; it's got our address on it.'

Alby glanced at it. 'Dr Alan Harrison,' he read out. 'Henley on Thames. The Harrisons of Henley. Has a nice ring. Might use it for the title of my first novel.'

'Hope you'll finish the sonnet first,' said Shirley.

'Never fear,' said Alby, 'it will be done before sunrise.'

'In that case you could let us have it before we leave,' said Shirley. 'We're not expecting daddy until around lunch time.'

'Great,' said Alby. 'Hope to see you in the morning

147

then. Now you'd both better go and get dry before you catch pneumonia.'

Beth gave me a smile as she and Shirley hurried up the short path and disappeared into the cottage.

'Since when were you able to write sonnets?' I said as we headed down the hill to the beach road.

'Alby grinned. 'Since I decided it could be our passport to a nice weekend in Henley. Maybe go down for the Regatta.'

'You're a devious blighter,' I said.

'Who me?' said Alby, looking skyward.

'By the way,' I said. 'how far did you go with Shirley before it started raining?'

He pretended to look shocked. 'A gentleman doesn't reveal such things, not even to his closest friend. Let's just say things reached an interesting point.'

By the time we arrived at the bottom of the hill the drizzle had stopped and the warmth from the sun had begun drying our clothes.

'Hope you're in the mood for a little sonnet writing,' Alby said after a while.

'You got yourself into that,' I said. 'It's up to you.'

'Well of course I could try adapting a bit of Shakespeare,' said Alby. 'I noticed a collection of his work in the bookcase at the flat. But maybe I| won't need him. I have beside me the kid who came top of the class in English Lit. I'd hate to deprive you of this chance to impress the girls.'

'Never written a poem in my life,' I said.

'Don't worry,' said Alby, 'I'll help if you get stuck. We should be able to cobble something together between us.'

When we got back to the flat the Wilsons were sitting at the window watching a ship moving slowly along the horizon.

'That's a destroyer if I'm not mistaken,' said Mr Wilson. 'Been a lot of Navy ships out there today. I reckon there's probably an exercise going on.'

'If you say so dear,' said his wife. Then she turned to Alby and me. 'I expect you're hungry. We've saved you some cheese and cucumber sandwiches.'

'Not for me thanks,' said Alby. 'A mug of tea would go down nicely though.'

'Are you sure that's all you want, dear?'

'Positive, mum.'

She looked concerned but didn't argue, then turned to me. 'I'm sure you'd like a sandwich, Matt.'

I said I'd love one.

After she had disappeared into the kitchenette, Mr Wilson turned to Alby. 'Not feeling too good, son?'

'Bit weary,' said Alby. 'We've been on a fair old hike.'

Mrs Wilson brought me a sandwich and a mug of tea   and I sat down to eat it at the table. Alby took his mug of tea and settled back in one of the armchairs. Within moments he was asleep, the mug balanced on an arm of the chair.

Mrs Wilson went over and picked up the mug, and stood looking at her son. 'Do him good to sleep for a while,' she said. 'He must need it.'

'Doesn't take a lot to tire him out these days,' said her husband.

Mrs Wilson nodded. 'He always had so much energy; I used to wonder where he got it from.'

When I'd finished my sandwich Mr Wilson pointed to a set of draughts lying on the window sill and suggested a game to pass the time until Alby woke up.

'Hope you're not a bandit like our Alby,' he said, with a flicker of a smile as he set up the board on the table. 'Haven't taken a game off him since last Christmas, and I have my suspicions he let me win that one.'

Mr Wilson narrowly won the first game, and we were well into the second when Alby woke up. He came over and watched us for a while as his father began eliminating my pieces, then he pulled up a chair beside mine.

'Can I advise my mate?' he said, looking across at his father.

'Not allowed,' said Mr Wilson.

'You mean I can't tell him to get those two pieces moving off the second row?'

'No, you can't.'

'Alright, I won't then.' Alby grinned.

Helped by a few more prompts from Alby, I managed to win the game with only three of my pieces left on the board.

Mr Wilson laughed ruefully. 'You really came back from the dead to take that one, Matt,' he said.

'I thought you were unlucky to lose, dad,' said a poker-faced Alby.

'Luck doesn't come into to it when you're around,' said Mr Wilson.

Alby laughed. 'Now Matt and me have got to go and write some poetry.'

Mr Wilson didn't look too surprised. He was used to his son's peccadillos.

Alby went over to the book case, ran his eye along the shelves and pulled out a thick red volume. 'Come on Matt, we've got work to do.'

'What's the book?' I asked as I followed him into our bedroom.

'The collected works of William Shakespeare.' Alby sat on his bed and began turning the pages. 'Here we are,' he said finally. 'The sonnets… This is the one I was looking for.' He began reading:

"Shall I compare thee to a summer's day?
Thou art more lovely and more temperate.
Rough winds do shake the darling buds of May,
And summer's lease hath all…"

'Hang on,' I interrupted, sitting down on the wicker chair. 'What have you got in mind?'

'I thought it might be just the thing for the girls,' said Alby. 'We'd have to change it round a bit, of course, update the language here and there'

'It's much too well-known,' I said. 'Wouldn't be surprised if Shirley and Beth know it by heart. I bet they go to one of those posh private schools where they stuff the kids' heads full of Shakespeare.'

Alby shrugged. 'You're probably right, but at least old Will should be able to give us a few ideas.' He began turning the pages of the book again. 'How about this?' he said:

"Full many a glorious morning have I seen
Flatter the mountain tops with sovereign eye
Kissing with golden face the meadows green,
Gliding pale streams…"

'A touch flowery for 1948 don't you think?' I said.

'Oh I don't know,' said Alby, 'there are some ideas

there I reckon we could work on.'

I said I thought the girls would probably laugh all the way back to Henley if we tried passing off a Shakespeare sonnet as our own, no matter how   much we doctored it.

Alby continued leafing through the book. 'Hey listen to this one,' he said after a while, and began reading out a sonnet full of allusions to death and corpses and graves and worms.

'You're not suggesting that kind of stuff would appeal to the girls?'

'Of course not, just thought you might find it amusing.'

'A real load of laughs,' I said.

'You have to remember when old Will was writing his stuff, folk were dying off like flies,' said Alby. 'They were always having epidemics, and there wasn't much in the way of medicines. Surgeons didn't realise they needed to wash their grubby hands before poking around inside people or sawing off arms and legs.'

'Yes,' I agreed, 'I believe it was a pretty dangerous time to be around.'

Alby nodded. 'If you met somebody you knew in the street you probably wouldn't say "Nice weather for the time of year" or "How are the kids?" You'd ask if they'd buried anyone since you last saw them.'

'They must have had other things they worried about,' I said.

Alby thought for a moment. 'Well I suppose they occasionally got fussed about things like the price of venison, the latest fashion in doublets and the lord of the manor having it off with one of his kitchen maids. But I'm

152

sure death was the big topic of conversation.'

'How bloody morbid,' I said.

'The trouble nowadays, people just don't like talking about death,' said Alby.

'There are jollier subjects,' I said.

'But dying's as much a part of everyday life as eating or going for a pee or fancying Betty Grable,' said Alby.

'Give me Betty Grable any time,' I said. 'Seeing Hetty Peck's body floating in the cut put me off death for life.'

'You're lucky we weren't kids when our grans were,' said Alby. 'It wasn't as bad as in Shakespeare's time, but people were still popping off all the time from diphtheria and TB and things like that. Families thought nothing of having corpses lying around the house for days on end. The relations would drop in for a cup of tea and then go and say their cheerios to whoever happening to be lying in the coffin. Thought nothing of it. These days the stiffs are whisked away before you can say Burke and Hare.'

'Would you fancy having a corpse lying nearby while you were having your dinner?' I wondered.

'You'd get used to it if it was the normal thing,' said Alby. 'Folk today would rather belch or fart than mention the word *death* in polite company. They talk about "passing on" or "going to a better place" or "finding peace". The poor bugger they're talking about might just as well have gone on holiday as been whisked off by the grim reaper. Hope we never pussyfoot around like that.'

'Of course we won't,' I said.

'Best mates need to be able to talk about things

straight on,' said Alby.

'No holds barred,' I said.

Alby looked at me steadily. 'This cancer lark sees off quite a few people, you know. Has it crossed your mind it could do for me?'

'I've tried not to think about that.'

'But it's crossed your mind?'

'Well yes, of course it has.'

'It's been crossing mine quite a bit,' said Alby. 'D'you know what I've decided? I'm going to give the lump a bloody good run for its money. There's too many things I want to have a dabble at before I cash in my chips.' His cheeks flushed. 'Anyway, sod cancer for now, we've got a sonnet to write.'

We sat scribbling on the scrap pads Mrs Wilson had thoughtfully provided for us to play games during the car journey. After a few minutes Alby said wearily, 'It's hard to get your mind onto this romantic stuff.'

'You have to concentrate,' I said.

'I know that,' said Alby, 'but on what.'

'Think about your perfect kind of girl,' I said. 'her eyes, her smile, her hair, her voice, those kind of things.'

'I know who you're thinking about,' said Alby.

I didn't answer.

For a few minutes the only sound in the room was the scratching of our pencils, then Alby broke the silence. 'I've only managed five lines so far, and they're more suitable for a rugger song than a lovey dovey poem. I'm going to have to leave it to you, mate.' He sank back on his bed into the feather pillows and closed his eyes. Soon he was sleeping like a baby.

I scribbled on until the aroma of frying sausages

began drifting into the room. It reminded me I was hungry, but also seemed to concentrate my mind. The lines began to flow, almost as if my hand was being guided by some unseen force. Finally I shook Alby awake and told him. 'I've finished the sonnet, except for the title.'

'I knew you'd manage it,' he said.

'Maybe the Big Fellah decided to help,' I said. 'The words just seemed to come into my head. Not sure if they're any good though.'

Alby sat up, leaning against the pillows. 'Sure you've got the right number of lines, and that rhyming couplet you're supposed to have at the end?'

'Yes,' I said, 'I've tried to do it the way old Will used to.'

Alby clapped his hands. 'Come on then, give your sonnet its world premiere.'

'No laughing or throwing up,' I said.

'Would I do something like that?' said Alby, his eyes wide with mock innocence.

'Remember now, sonnets are meant to be pretty schmaltzy,' I said. I read slowly but with   a touch of the dramatic, the way I imagined Miss Dowdeswell might do it:

A precious moment engraved in time
When we met upon that sunlit shore,
True beauty in a world of pantomime.
Being with you made my spirits soar.
Your smiles would light the greyest day
And cast a golden glow across the hills.
Your humour and your endearing ways
Could surely bend a thousand wills.
Melancholy isn't in your repertoire.

I'll think of you as each day starts.
You'll always be my shining star
And from now on my Queen of Hearts.
Our time together was all too brief,
For me it was a mere aperitif.

'Blimey,' said Alby, 'you sure you haven't cribbed that from the Bleeding Hearts Handbook?'

'Think it's too mushy?' I said.

'Might be just the ticket,' said Alby. 'How d'you dream up stuff like that?'

'Funny really,' I said, 'once I got going it didn't seem to be me writing it. The pencil just moved over the paper like it was taking down dictation from somebody.'

'Trouble is,' said Alby, 'it doesn't sound like the kind of stuff a kid from a council estate would come up with. The girls'll probably think it was pinched from some old poetry book.'

'I doubt it,' I said, 'they're too smart for that. They'll probably recognise straight away it's just a bit of half-baked dabbling.'

Before Alby could respond we heard his mother calling us for dinner.

After we had dined on sausage and mash followed by tinned peaches and Cornish ice cream, we went back into the bedroom to go over the sonnet once more. As Alby had the neatest handwriting, he wrote out the final version with the heading *My Shining Star,* and placed it in an envelope we found in a drawer. On the cover he wrote *For Shirley and Beth.*

'I thought the sonnet was supposed to be from you to Shirley,' I said.

'Nah, I couldn't take the credit, mate,' said Alby.

'It's all your work.'

'You've addressed it to both girls,' I said.

'I reckon that's only fair,' said Alby, 'and I'll tell them who the author was.'

'The next morning after breakfast we took the now familiar route across Polzeath beach and up the cliff path towards Daymer Bay and Rock. A strong breeze was whipping up the Atlantic rollers and chasing woolly puffs of cloud across the sky. Out in the bay a scattering of fishing boats were bobbing around like toys in a child's bath.

On the flat grassy hinterland back from the cliffs children were flying kites, laughing and shouting as they tried to control them in the swirling gusts. One small boy's box kite had lodged in the branches of a tree just over a wall in the grounds of a private hotel. We watched as his mother vainly tried to pull the kite free. Then Alby strode over, levered himself onto the wall and managed to reach up into the branches and release the kite. We stood for a while watching as the boy ran back and forth, causing the kite to gyrate and swoop, and flirt once more with the tree.

'Come on,' said Alby, 'let's push on before he gets his kite snarled up again. I haven't got the puff to repeat my white knight act.'

By the time we reached the cottage where Shirley and Beth had been staying, it was nearing eleven o'clock. Before we could knock on the door it was opened by an elderly lady. 'Good morning,' she said pleasantly. 'You'll be the young gentlemen my nieces said might be calling. I'm awfully sorry but you've just missed them. Their father came to collect them a little earlier than expected. He had to get back to Henley for some meeting or other. Shirley and Beth said to apologise.'

We thanked her and as we turned to leave, she asked, 'Is there any message I can pass on?'

Alby hesitated. 'No, it's okay thanks. We have their address if we want to get in touch.'

'Enjoy the rest of your holiday,' said the old lady.

As we strolled back down the lane I asked Alby if he wanted to post the sonnet to the twins.

'Up to you mate,' he said. 'You're the author.'

'I'll think about it,' I said, but I was already pondering the possibility of rewriting it for Helen O'Donnell. After all, I'd had her in my mind while I was composing it. I doubted though, I'd be able to summon up the nerve to give it to her.

Alby suggested we follow a different route back to Polzeath, one which took us around the lanes through the village of Trebetherick. After we had walked for a while we became aware of an aroma of fresh baked bread and something delightfully savoury. Almost involuntarily our stride quickened and soon we came upon a small bakery shop.

'Have to investigate that great smell,' said Alby, and led the way into the shop.

A young woman behind the counter asked, 'What can I get you?'

'Whatever's giving off that lovely aroma,' said Alby

'Oh that's the pasties,' said the woman. 'We've just made a fresh batch.'

'We'll have two,' said Alby, fishing out a half crown from his pocket.

As we headed out of the shop he handed one of the

158

pasties to me. I couldn't remember ever feeling hungrier than at that moment. Even Alby, whose appetite had recently diminished, admitted to salivating. As we walked on towards Trebetherick we munched through the crusty pastry, bulging with succulent meat, potatoes and onions. We agreed it was hard to imagine anything tasting better.

Despite our disappointment at missing Beth and Shirley, the delicious pasties and the warm sunshine raised our spirits. We were soon embarked on our own version of *She'll Be Coming Round the Mountain,* in which each verse became ruder than the one before. At the top of the steep hill running down into Polzeath village we stopped for a breather, sitting on a grassy bank beside the road. Alby leaned back against a low stone wall and closed his eyes. 'I think we should forget about sending the sonnet to Shirley and Beth,' he said.

'I agree,' I said, 'but what's your reason?'

'Doesn't seem much point. I don't think we'll be seeing the girls again.'

'I thought you wanted to keep in touch and maybe wangle a visit to Henley.'

'Been thinking about that,' said Alby. 'We hardly know the girls really. What would we say to them? Lovely to see you again... wasn't it fun in Polzeath... how about a smooch? And anyway, if a couple of rough diamonds like us turned up on his doorstep, their old man would probably offer us a bowl of soup and a few coppers and send us packing.'

I couldn't help wondering if Alby had another, sadder reason for scrapping any idea of going to Henley, a reason to do with his uncertainty about what lay in store for him in the days ahead. I hadn't the heart to ask him. We didn't talk much during the rest of the walk back to the flat, though we did invent a few more rude verses for the mountain song.

The weather grew even warmer after Beth and Shirley had left and Alby and me spent most of the remaining days of the holiday swimming or lying on the beach, reading and gossiping and playing mind games. When the beach got crowded we would walk along the cliffs to the stretch of coastline called The Rumps. There we would find a quiet spot away from the coastal path and lie in the soft, springy grass watching the passing boats and the seals frolicking in the swell among the rocky outcrops out in the bay.

The days seemed to slip by almost as if we were in a dream. Our talk and our imaginings roamed anywhere and everywhere. Sometimes we would see who could conjure up the most bizarre scenarios; an oasis in the middle of the Sahara with a 24-table snooker hall, a nightclub on the summit of Mount Everest with Miss Dowdeswell doing a striptease act, or a football stadium at the centre of the earth with two teams of troglodytes contesting the Subterranean FA Cup Final. At other times we would re-live the adventures of our favourite comic book heroes.

On the day before we were to go home we went back for a final visit to our favourite spot on The Rumps. The sea was calm and the morning sun gave a shimmering edge to the incoming rollers. We lay gazing out across the water and spotted what looked like an oil tanker disappearing slowly to the west.

'Where do you think that tanker was heading?'

'No idea,' I said. 'France, America maybe.'

'How'd you like to go to America some day?'

'Never thought about it.'

'I have,' said Alby. 'I really fancy it. That's if I get over this lot.' He tapped his abdomen.

'Cost you a packet to get there,' I said.

Alby shrugged. 'Wouldn't need to go on one of those fancy passenger liners. Get a berth on a tramp steamer, down with the cargo on the lower deck. That ought to be pretty cheap.'

'Maybe you could work your passage as a cabin boy or cook's helper or a lookout or something,' I suggested. 'Think I'd need to come as well though, to keep you out of trouble.'

'Of course, I wouldn't go without you,' said Alby. 'Be great to go together, and make our fortunes.'

'Yes,' I said, 'I reckon it would.'

'That's settled then,' said Alby. 'So long as the Big Fellah doesn't have other plans for me.'

We spent the next two hours or more day-dreaming about the exciting adventures we would have in America before finally settling down and becoming rich.

That night I had a long talk with the Big Fellah about Alby and his lump, and how much my pal would have to offer the world if he was given the chance. Before I said 'amen', I begged Him, even if he never listened to me again, to listen this time. I reminded him the next day as we headed home, and many more times in the days that followed.

CHAPTER FIFTEEN

Two days after we got home from Cornwall Alby took a turn for the worse and was taken into the General Hospital late at night. It was the following weekend before   anyone other than his immediate family were permitted to visit him.

When finally, on the Saturday afternoon, I was allowed into the hospital with his mum and dad, Alby was sitting up reading. As he spotted us approaching I saw him slip the book under his pillow. He looked haggard and pale, but the old alertness was still there in his eyes.

'How're you feeling, love?' his mother inquired.

'Not quite ready for running a marathon,' he said, rubbing his midriff.

His mum and dad sat down on the chairs either side and I sat on the end of the bed.

'What have the doctors had to say?' asked Mr Wilson.

'Not a lot,' said Alby. 'I've found out a lot more from reading my notes.'

'Are you supposed to look at those?' said Mrs Wilson.

'Why not?' said Alby. 'It's me they're writing about. Anyway, if they leave the file at the end of your bed, what can they expect?'

'But you could easily get the wrong end of the stick if you don't properly understand all the medical jargon,' said Mr Wilson.

'Not if you've done your homework,' said Alby.
'I've had a couple of useful visits to the library between my
sessions in here.'

Mrs Wilson shook her head. 'Honestly Alby, do
you really think you should be filling your head with all
that medical stuff.'

'I like to know what's going on inside my carcass,'
said Alby.

'Of course you do dear,' said Mrs Wilson. 'It's just
that I don't want you to be worrying unnecessarily.'

'Everybody in this place spends their day
worrying,' said Alby. 'Helps pass the time.'

'The nurse at the desk told us your consultant
wanted a word with us while we're here,' said Mr Wilson.

'That'll be Doc Tully,' said Alby. 'He's all right.
Talks like he's got a plum in his mouth, but he knows his
stuff. He'll put the best gloss he can on what he tells you,
and won't give much away. He doesn't like confusing his
patients' relatives with a lot of medical guff he thinks they
mightn't properly understand.'

Mrs Wilson reached down and produced a bottle of
lemon barley water and a packet of Crawfords' assorted
biscuits from a shopping bag and placed them on Alby's
bedside locker. 'Almost forgot these love,' she said.
'Anything special you'd like next time?'

'No thanks, mum,' he said. 'You've already brought
in enough to keep the ward fed for a week.'

Mrs Wilson patted his arm. 'Well you did say you
weren't keen on the hospital food.'

'That's because I've been spoiled with such great
grub at home,' said Alby. Mr Wilson nodded his agreement
and his wife beamed.

163

'See that bloke over there,' said Alby, nodding towards an emaciated white-haired man in the bed opposite, 'he thinks he's got bronchitis. Everybody else in the place knows he's got lung cancer. Nice old buffer, but a bit forgetful, and never gets any visitors.'

'The poor man,' said Mrs Wilson. 'But you can understand the doctors not always wanting to tell patients the whole truth. Can't do a lot of good frightening them.'

'I'd get really brassed off if they tried to bamboozle me,' said Alby.

'But you're different,' said his mother.

I couldn't think of anyone who would disagree with Mrs Wilson's assessment of her son.

'I've found out from the quacks exactly what kind of cancer I've got,' said Alby.

'Are there different types then?' I asked.

'More varieties than you could shake a stick at,' said Alby. 'None of them are too pleasant, but some are nastier than others. The statistics aren't too jolly if you get the wrong kind.'

Mr and Mrs Wilson glanced at each other. 'I think perhaps we ought to go and see if that consultant's available,' said Mr Wilson.

'Don't be too put off by his posh voice,' said Alby. 'He goes greyhound racing and has a season ticket for the Blues.'

As his parents walked off down the ward, Alby shook his head with a wry smile. 'Mum always gets a bit embarrassed talking to toffs.' He eased himself up on the pillows. 'Now come on mate, cheer me up. You look like you're just about to go into a maths exam on a wet Monday morning.'

164

'Sorry,' I said. 'These places give me the willies.'

'Not too keen on them myself,' said Alby, 'but they can't make them too cosy or you'd have every tramp in the district finding excuses to come in for a kip and free grub.'

'What were those statistics you were talking about?'

'Didn't want to upset the folks with them,' said Alby, 'but I've found out that punters with my particular kind of cancer have about a ten to fifteen percent chance at best of coming through it.'

'I'm sure you'll be in the fifteen per cent,' I said.

'As a betting man I'd want better odds if I was putting money on myself,' said Alby. 'But it's all up to the Big Fellah. Anyway, let's skip the doom and gloom stuff for now, I could do with a laugh.'

'What was that book you shoved under the pillow when we came in?' I asked.

Alby pulled out a slim volume and held it up. '*The Kama Sutra.* One of the blokes in the ward lent it me.'

'What's it about?'

Alby waved a finger and grinned. 'Not really suitable for an innocent young chap like you,' he said. 'It's a kind of handbook for contortionists who're keen on the ladies. Here, take a peek.'

I flicked through the pages. 'See what you mean. Better stick it back under your pillow before your folks come back.'

'Don't worry,' said Alby, 'I'm going to give it back to the guy who lent it to me after you've gone. It's okay for a laugh, but I got a *John Buchan* off the book trolley this morning; more the kind of thing you need to get your mind off things in this fun palace.'

'What have they been doing to you this week?'

'Pills, injections, more blasts of radiation.' He grimaced, 'Wouldn't be surprised if they started pulling out my toenails next.'

'The treatment must be doing you some good,' I said.

'Can't be sure,' said Alby. 'The quacks are always a bit cagey about how you're doing, unless they can tell you you're definitely improving.'

'What have they told you?'

'Not as much as I'd like. There's quite a few things I want to check out in the medical books when I get the chance.'

'Not sure I'd want to know all the gruesome details if it was me,' I said.

'Don't believe in letting the quacks pull the wool over my eyes,' said Alby. 'I like to… look out, here comes the medicine trolley.'

The nurse who had been trundling the trolley down the ward stopped beside Alby's bed and handed him a small paper cup containing three tablets. 'Your afternoon treat, Alby,' she said. 'Don't forget to have plenty of water with them.'

'I won't,' he said. After she had gone he placed the tablets on his locker beside a half-full glass of water.

'Aren't you going to take the pills? I said.

Alby nodded. 'When I'm ready. Mustn't be too obedient. Have to try and keep a bit of independence in these places. Anyway, how're your folks?'

'Okay,' I said. 'They sent their best.'

'Your mum got that cough sorted out yet?'

'She seems to be stuck with it,' I said. 'The doc says it's bronchitis and em something or other.'

166

'Emphysema,' said Alby. 'Buggers up your lungs. That's why your mum's always puffing and wheezing.' He shook his head, smiling. 'We're bloody lucky with our mums. Two from the top drawer. Be nice to pay them back one day. Properly I mean; take them on holiday somewhere really plush like the French Riviera, buy them a few fancy frocks and a little car apiece to drive themselves around. And when we really make a pile we could get them both a big house up by Chamberlain Park.'

'Do you really reckon we'll be rich one day?' I said.

'Of course,' said Alby. 'Just a matter of time.' Before he could expound further his mum and dad came back, trying without much success to look cheerful.

'Well, what little gems did Dr Tully have to offer?' Alby asked.

'He was very nice,' said Mrs Wilson, 'but I'm not sure I understood all the things he told us.'

'You should have asked him to explain,' said Alby.

'I wouldn't want to show my ignorance in front of such an educated gentleman,' said Mrs Wilson.

'What he did make clear,' said Mr Wilson, 'is that you're getting the best treatment available.'

Alby's mum nodded and her face brightened. 'And he said you should be able to come home again in a few days.'

'Yes, I know,' said Alby. 'I've got to have a bit more radiation first. They allow a lot of their customers to go home between treatments. More comings and goings in this ward than at that knocking shop on Victoria Road.'

'Alby!' said Mrs Wilson, looking suitably shocked.

'Sorry, mum,' he said, giving his dad and me a

wink.

'We can't wait to have you home again, love,' said Mrs Wilson.

Her husband nodded and squeezed her hand. I felt like doing the same, but made do with a promise to call round as soon as Alby was home.

CHAPTER SIXTEEN

After Alby was allowed home from the hospital there were still two weeks of the school holidays left, and I went round to his house as often as I could. Sometimes we were joined by Tubbo Simms, Dipper Dickson and occasionally other pals for a game of Poker or Monopoly.

Alby's illness didn't seem to diminish his winning touch. He carried on relieving us of our pocket money, still doing it with his usual good humour, so that we almost didn't mind. But on the last Saturday afternoon before school term was due to begin a session of Stud Poker ended with three of us winning a little cash while Alby was the only loser.

After Dipper and Tubbo had gone home for tea, Alby smiled the knowing smile I knew so well. 'You all did well today,' he said.

'Only as well as you let us,' I said, convinced that the game had ended exactly the way he intended.

Alby laughed. 'You never know; maybe the Wilson system isn't foolproof.'

'It seems to have been up to now,' I said as I got up to leave.

'All good things have to come to an end some time,' said Alby.

As I headed home I pondered his parting words and, given the nature of his illness, they began to take on a rather ominous significance. I wondered why he had chosen to be the loser in the Poker session and allowed everyone else to win? Did he simply have a sudden generous impulse, or could it be that he feared this might be the last time he expected to play cards with his friends, and he ought to let us recoup a little of our losses?

The question was still playing on my mind as I strolled on in the gathering dusk. Turning into the dimly lit alleyway which provided a short-cut from Victoria Road to Jubilee Avenue I could see four figures approaching from the opposite direction. By the time I realised it was Frankie Beckett and three of his cronies it was too late to turn back.

'Well look who we have here,' said Frankie as we came face to face. Lenny Bradd, Mick Golding and another lad who I recognised from Sharkey Road crowded round me.

'This is the chance you've been waiting for, Frankie,' said Mick.

Frankie nodded. 'Yeh, and I'll handle it my way.'

'We'll keep a lookout,' said the boy whose name I didn't know.

'No,' said Frankie, 'I want to do this on my own. You three get off home.'

'You sure?' said Lenny.

'Dead sure,' said Frankie. 'Now go.'

'Don't want any witnesses eh?' said Mick.

'See you tomorrow,' said Frankie.

As the three Sharkeys ambled off I though of making a run for it, but I knew that even if I got away I would have to face Frankie sooner or later. I decided I'd endured enough of living in fear of meeting him, and that delaying the inevitable confrontation would probably prove more painful than facing up to it now.

As Frankie turned to face me I felt not fear but a kind of numb acceptance that I was about to suffer the kind of pain I'd experienced that night when we fought over the

170

football tickets. I was surprised when Frankie stepped back and said, 'You're expecting me to beat the crap out of you, aren't you?'

'It had crossed my mind,' I said.

Frankie took out a cigarette, lit it and blew the smoke upwards. 'Well, I'm not going to lay a hand on you.'

'But I thought you... '

'Yeh I've been wanting to give you a bloody belting.'

'What changed your mind.'

'Your mate, Alby Wilson.'

'I don't understand.'

'Met him at the hospital. I was in for a check-up. They like to keep an eye on you for a bit when you've had concussion. I bumped into Alby. He'd just been for radiation treatment. He looked terrible. Told me about his cancer. Uncle of mine had the same kind and was a goner a month after they found it. I didn't tell Alby, but I don't fancy his chances.'

'Alby didn't mention he'd met you at the hospital,' I said.

'Then he won't have told you about the little agreement he talked me into.'

'What was that?'

'Asked me, as a special favour to him, to lay off you. I nearly told him to get lost, but I managed to bite my tongue. You might think I'm a hard bastard, but even hard bastards don't refuse a dying kid a favour. You'd better not go blabbing about this round the school though. If you did I'd have to sort you out.'

'I won't say anything,' I said, 'but when Mick and Lenny and the rest of your mates see me they'll wonder

171

why I haven't got a mark on me.'

Frankie nodded. 'That's a point. Maybe I'd better slap you around a bit. Nah, I suppose that'd be ratting on Alby. I'll just say I made sure your bruises are where they don't show.'

I put out my hand to shake with Frankie but he ignored it. 'I shan't forget what you did to me. Just remember the only reason you're not a hospital case yourself tonight is because your mate is dying.'

As we walked off in different directions, the only thing I was sure of was that I would cheerfully have accepted the worst beating Frankie could have given me to have Alby well again.

CHAPTER SEVENTEEN

I slept badly after my confrontation with Frankie, unable to get Alby out of my mind. The next morning, as soon as I'd finished my breakfast, I hurried round to his house, but there was no answer to my repeated knocking. Mrs Froggatt from next-door must have heard me and she came out wearing a dressing gown.

'They're at the hospital,' she said. 'An ambulance came for Alby last night. Near midnight it was.'

I thanked her and, not for the first time, was struck by how the mournful local accent made worrying news seem even more alarming.

Around two o'clock I went round to Alby's again, but there was still no-one home. I decided to try once more in the early evening. This time I found the Wilsons just leaving to return to the hospital.

'Alby had a really bad turn,' said Mrs Wilson, her eyes red-rimmed. 'We had to call an ambulance.'

'How is he now?' I asked.

'He was sleeping when we left the hospital,' said Mr Wilson. 'I think they'd given him some pretty strong knockout drops.'

I asked if I could go with them to the hospital.

'Sorry Matt,' said Mr Wilson. 'I know Alby would love to see you, but the doctors have restricted visitors again to next of kin. We'll let you know if it changes.'

The first few days of the new school term dragged slower than any period in my life. Each evening after my paper round I called at Alby's house to find out how he was, but the news was always the same. He remained very poorly. It was on the second Friday of the new term that I got the news I had been waiting for. I would be allowed to visit Alby the next day.

I arrived at the General Hospital half an hour before the visiting period and had to sit outside the cancer ward until the appointed time. When I hurried into the ward where I'd visited Alby previously there was no sign of him in any of the beds. Fearing the worst, I almost ran to the nurses' station to ask where he was. I could have kissed the sister-in-charge when she told me that he had just been moved into a room on his own. She directed me along a short corridor leading off the ward and said I would find Alby in the room at the end.

As I approached I could see him through the glass door lying watching a drip hooked up to his arm. I pushed open the door and he glanced up. 'Just the bloke I need to see,' he said.

'They wouldn't let me come until now,' I said.

'I know,' he said. 'I told them you'd probably do me more good than half a dozen blasts of radiation, but they reckon they know best.'

'Why have they moved you into a room on your own?' I asked.

He smiled faintly. 'They realised what an important patient I am.'

'Of course you are,' I said, 'but what's the real reason?'

'Probably because they've decided I'll soon be a goner,' said Alby. 'Think they prefer their patients to conk out quietly in one of these private rooms rather than in the

174

main ward, so it doesn't upset the rest of the customers.'

'For goodness sake, Alby,' I said, 'you're not going to…'

'To die?' he interjected. 'I'm not planning to, at least not just yet. Trouble is the bloody hand grenade in here has been firing off bits around my body, and they've landed up in some awkward places. I get the impression the quacks are a bit more worried than they let on.'

'What makes you think that?'

'Watching their faces, listening to the way they lower their voices when they pay me a visit on their rounds, seeing how the nurses make a lot more fuss of me than before.'

'They still giving you that radiation treatment?'

'A regular dose after breakfast.'

'What's it like?'

'Don't feel anything at the time. Afterwards you can feel a bit knackered. Sometimes they pump some fresh blood into you to perk you up.'

'Hope they know what they're doing,' I said. 'When you think what radiation did to the Japanese folk who had the atom bombs dropped on them…'

'The quacks are pretty careful,' said Alby. 'They don't want their patients melting down like in Hiroshima. Anyway, enough jolly hospital stuff, I want to hear what's going on outside. You're still in one piece. That must mean you haven't had a dust up with Frankie Beckett yet.'

'I met him the other night,' I said. 'He told me about you persuading him to leave me alone. Why didn't you tell me?'

'I would have done,' said Alby, 'but I wasn't sure

whether Frankie would keep his word.'

'Anyway, thanks,' I said.

Alby grinned. 'What are mates for?'

'All your pals in the Fifth sent their best,' I said.

'The Fifth, eh. Of course, you're all Fifth Formers now.'

'So will you be when you've finished in here.'

'Yeh, of course I will.'

'Dipper and Tubbo and some of the others wanted to come and visit you,' I said, 'but I told them the hospital wouldn't allow a mob like them in. Be too tiring for you.'

'You're as bad as my mum, the way you fuss over me,' said Alby.

'Somebody has to keep an eye on you.'

'Funny,' he said, 'I always reckoned to be the one who looked out for you. Saw myself as a bit of a guardian angel, I suppose.'

'Never thought of you as an angel.'

'Hope the Big Fellah doesn't either,' said Alby, 'at least not for a while.'

'Can't see any wings sprouting,' I said.

Alby felt his shoulder blades. 'No, nothing happening at the moment. Which, for some daft reason, reminds me; I was wondering how'd you like to inherit the Albert Wilson infallible system for winning at cards and Monopoly?'

'I don't want to inherit anything,' I said. 'I'd just like you to get better.'

'But in case the Big Fellah does decide he needs my services upstairs, you might find my system quite a handy little earner.'

'Wish you'd stop talking like that.'

176

'Thought we'd agreed there was nothing we couldn't talk about together.'

'Yes, but...' I began.

'No buts,' Alby interjected. 'There's an envelope in my locker with your name on it. Inside there's all you need to know about my system. Of course you'll only get it if the Big Fellah sends for me.'

I tried again to protest, but Alby raised his hand like a policeman halting traffic. 'It's okay, mate, I've never seen the point of whistling in the dark.'

'You know what?' I said. 'Best friends ought to be immortal.'

'I'd go along with that,' said Alby. 'I'll suggest it to the Big Fellah when I meet him, but for now, could you pass me the bed pan from the locker cupboard.'

I handed him the pan and he slipped it under the bedclothes. He winced as he began using it.

'The old dingaling's bloody tender. They stuck a metal thing up it yesterday to check the state of my bladder.' When he'd finished he rang for a nurse.

A pert, dark-haired young nurse appeared and asked cheerily, 'What can I do for you, Alby?'

Alby grinned. 'That's what I think they call a leading question.'

The nurse shook her head, smiling. 'Behave yourself young man.'

'You know I'm a perfect gentleman, Maggie,' he said. 'My best friend, Matt here, will confirm it.'

The nurse tittered.

'Anyway, I've got a little present for you, Maggie,' he said, handing her the bed pan.

'Is it still hurting when you go,' she said.

177

'A bit,' said Alby.

'It'll get easier in a day or two,' she said.

As the nurse went off with the pan, Alby watched her and smiled. 'Almost worth putting up with an uncomfortable pee just to watch her take it away,' he said. 'Smashing little bottom don't you think? Takes your mind off things. Trouble with these places, you get too much time to think.   Lot of daft thoughts go through your head.'

'What kind of thoughts?' I asked.

'Like "Why me?" and "I'm too young for this kind of carry-on" and "Did I do something to upset the Big Fellah?" Have a gab with him most nights, but sometimes it's hard to think what to say. I mean, you can't really ask him to give you special consideration over all the other folk in here. And it would be pretty pathetic to promise that if he let you off the hook you'd stop being an uppity sod and start behaving like Saint Francis.'

'No good promising the impossible,' I agreed.

'What I should be doing,' said Alby, 'is asking the Big Fellah to help some of the poor buggers in the other rooms along the corridor. One of them's close to suffocating 'cause the cancer's eaten most of his lungs away, and another's got feeding tubes up his nose because there's a lump nearly as big as a cricket ball in his mouth. Not a lot the quacks can do for them.'

'I'm sure their families are saying prayers for them,' I said.

'Hope so,' said Alby. 'Do a lot more good than all the bloody orange squash and sweets and crossword puzzle books they keeping bringing in.' He lay back on the raised pillows and closed his eyes.

After a while I said quietly, 'Are you going to sleep,

mate?'

'No, just doing a bit of daydreaming,' he said.

'What about?'

'All sorts of things; Cornwall for one. Remember those afternoons on the cliffs at Polzeath?'

'Of course I do.'

'And us planning to go to America.'

'Yes.'

'Well, I think I ought to tell you I've gone off the idea of becoming a film star. Got to thinking it's a bit of a poncy job.'

'I wouldn't call Humphrey Bogart or James Cagney poncy,' I said. 'At least not to their faces.'

'I'm not saying all actors are like that,' said Alby, 'but there's some, specially in those singing and dancing films, I wouldn't want to turn my back on while I was lacing up my shoes.'

'If you've gone off acting, what do you fancy doing if we go to America?' I asked.

He stroked his chin and stared into the middle distance. 'Private eye, Greyhound bus driver, cattle rancher maybe... No, I've got a better idea. We could become hoboes, ride the freight trains, have a good look around the place, then decide where to settle down and become millionaires.'

'I fancy the sound of that,' I said.

'Will you go on your own if I'm not around to go with you?' Alby asked.

'You'll be around,' I said.

Alby looked upwards. 'Are you listening, Big Fellah?' Then he turned to me. 'I've got to tell you about this dream I had last night, or it might have been yesterday

179

afternoon - lose track of the time with all the dope they keep pumping into me. There I was flying across the night sky heading towards the stars, no wings, not even a rocket up my backside, couldn't hear a sound or feel anything, and the stars kept getting brighter and brighter the further I went. Suddenly they all just seemed to merge into one great light, so bright I couldn't look at it. Know what, I reckon the Big Fellah was giving me a peek of heaven.'

'Hope it's got a bit more than bright light,' I said.

Alby thought for a moment. 'I suppose it needs to show up well in the dark so the souls of folk who die at night can find their way there.'

'Wonder what it's like?' I said.

'The Big Fellah must have to lay on some pretty good attractions to keep the residents happy,' said Alby. 'Eternity's a long time to be stuck in one place, and there must be quite a population up there when you think how many people have kicked the bucket over the centuries. And then there's all the animals and insects as well.'

'What sort of attractions do you reckon it has?' I asked.

'Probably have snooker halls with perfect tables, free swimming pools and cinemas, race courses where the bookies always lose, help-yourself fish and chip shops… and I'd hope there'd be a total ban on cricket.'

'Bet there's plenty of churches,' I said.

'I wouldn't be so sure,' said Alby. 'Not much left to pray for once you've got to heaven. I mean, you're already saved and I imagine your sins have all been forgiven. Everything's taken care of. Shouldn't think the Big Fellah would expect you to keep on thanking him and singing his praises.'

'Would you reckon the residents are able to put in a good word for their families and pals down here?' I wondered.

'I should think so,' said Alby. 'They must be bumping into the Big Fellah all the time. I can think of quite a few little requests I'd want to put to him, always assuming I don't get shipped off to the other place. I'd ask him to sort out the problem between our dads for a start, make Gran Ryder's lumbago a bit easier, and see our mums okay... oh and watch that Stan the Spiv treats our Enid properly.'

'I like your shopping list,' I said, 'but I hope you don't get chance to use it for a bloody long time yet.'

'I'm with you there,' said Alby, 'but the truth is none of us know when the Big Fellah will call us up. I reckon it's best to be prepared for all possibilities. Whenever I do get up there, d'you know one of the first things I'll do?'

'You'll probably need a pee after such a long journey,' I said.

Alby nodded. 'After that I'll track down my Grandad Ryder and take him for a game of snooker if he fancies it. I was only five when the Big Fellah whisked him off, and there's loads of stuff I'd like to ask him about. I'd look up Hetty Peck as well and explain about nicking that fruit from her shop. I might even have a gander at what Miss Dowdeswell gets up to after school hours.' He sank back against the pillows and yawned.

'Have a kip if you feel like it,' I said.

He didn't reply. His eyelids fluttered and closed, but this time he wasn't daydreaming. He was asleep. Fast asleep. I checked there was no-one around and gave him a

181

kiss on his forehead before tiptoeing away.

CHAPTER EIGHTEEN

Alby's mum and dad were called to the hospital in the early hours of the next morning. The doctors didn't think he would make it through the day. He did, but during the next two days his condition fluctuated between grave and desperate.

Maybe it was better I wasn't allowed to see Alby at that stage. I might have said some things that would have made him cringe, like telling him I loved him. He would probably have laughed and said 'Bollocks!' but he would have known I didn't mean it in a poncy way. I had no doubt at all he felt the same towards me, though I guess he would have burned his Monopoly board rather than admit it. As it was I didn't get the opportunity to embarrass Alby and he didn't have to do any burning.

One of the kids from the Froggatt family, the Wilsons' next-door neighbours, knocked on our door while we were having tea. He brought a message asking me to go round to the Wilsons as soon as I could. I didn't ask the messenger if he knew what it was about. I felt certain of the news that awaited me.

The sun was slipping away behind the factories on the edge of the estate as I hurried round to the Wilsons' house. I tried to think of what I would say to them and how I would stop myself from breaking down and upsetting them even more than they must already be.

Mr Wilson answered my knock on the door and ushered me in with an arm around my shoulder. 'Sit down,

Matt,' he said nodding towards the sofa. 'Alby's mum is making a cup of tea.' Mr Wilson sat beside me on the sofa and stared into the flickering flames of the fire. 'I expect you realise why we asked you to come round.'

'I think so,' I said.

'Alby died just after two o'clock this afternoon. We were with him. He went very peacefully at the end.'

Somehow I held back the tears, but couldn't find any words to say. I just nodded dumbly.

Mrs Wilson came into the room carrying a small tray with three cups of tea on it. 'Hello Matt,' she said in little more than a whisper. She placed the tray on the occasional table in front of the sofa and handed cups to her husband and myself before sitting down in an armchair beside us. She looked at me with the affection I always felt from her. 'Cliff has told you…' she said.

'Yes,' I said. I felt I ought to have said something more, but no words would come.

'We know how much you and Alby cared about each other,' said Mrs Wilson.

'He's my best friend,' I said. 'Always has been, always will be.'

'That's why we wanted to ask you to do something special at his funeral,' said Mr Wilson.

Mrs Wilson nodded. 'We'd like you to read the lesson.'

'I'd be honoured,' was all I could think of to say. Then, as I thought about it, I began to wonder if I would be able to get through the reading without finishing up in tears.

Mr Wilson said they would let me know as soon as the funeral arrangements had been made.

'I hope your mum and dad will both be able to come too,' said Mrs Wilson.

'I'm sure they'll want to,' I said. 'They thought the world of Alby.' I wasn't so sure though my father would be willing to attend.

As I was leaving, Mrs Wilson said, 'Just a minute Matt, I have something for you.' She went over to the sideboard and opened a drawer from which she took out an envelope and handed it to me. 'We found this in Alby's locker after he died.' The envelope bore my name in Alby's handwriting.

'I think I know what's in it,' I said.

'Oh,' said Mrs Wilson, looking puzzled.

'It's some information Alby wanted me to have.'

'Something private between the two of you?'

'Just some tips for playing cards and Monopoly,' I said.

She allowed herself a faint smile. 'I hope he wasn't trying to turn you into a card sharp.'

'No.' I said, 'I think he felt I lose too often and needed a bit of help.'

Both she and Mr Wilson gave me a hug before I left. Tears were welling up in her eyes, but I managed to hold myself together.

As I walked home I was tempted to open the envelope and read its contents. I took it from my coat pocket and looked at it, then put it away again. Somehow I couldn't raise any interest in a system for winning at cards or Monopoly. At that moment I felt like one of life's all-time losers.

CHAPTER NINETEEN

Alby's funeral service took place on a cloudless Saturday afternoon in late September at St Margaret's Church where he had been christened, and where just a few months earlier we had watched his sister Enid's marriage.

It was the first time since my Gran Sheridan's funeral five years before that I had been inside a church accompanied by both my parents. My worry that my father might not attend had thankfully proved unfounded. When he heard about the service he insisted on going. 'Whatever's gone on between me and Cliff Wilson had nothing to do with Alby,' he said.

When my mother said she was sure the Wilsons would be pleased to see him at the funeral, my father shrugged. 'That's as may be, but I'm only going because of the lad.'

We got to the church early and Alby's Uncle Wally, one of two ushers patrolling the entrance, directed us to a pew just behind the rows reserved for the Wilson family at the front. My mother sat between my father and me. As she and I bowed our heads in silent prayers, I was aware of my father staring straight ahead and upwards at the stained glass windows depicting Christ on the cross.

I tried to think of a proper, respectful prayer to say to the Big Fellah about Alby but the only words that came into my head were, 'Thank you for letting me be his friend. It would be great if all kids could have a friend like Alby. Please let him be happy living with you. And help me through my bible reading without blubbing.' Then, with my eyes still closed, I had this vision of a freckled-faced lad striding down the aisle of the church, his gap-toothed grin as wide as ever. He hops up onto the altar steps, turns to face the congregation, raises both thumbs, and addresses the congregation: 'Sorry you're going to have to put up with some boring stuff for the next half hour folks. Don't feel bad if you'd rather be somewhere else. I'm sure the Big Fellah would understand. After this lot's over I'm off for a game of snooker. Wish I could ask you to join me. On second thoughts I expect you'd probably rather not be able to just yet.'

As I opened my eyes, I felt my mother's hand gently touching my arm. 'Are you okay, love?' she asked.

'Yes,' I said. 'I'm fine.'

I looked around the church and felt comforted by the many familiar faces. In the pews ahead of us I recognised a lot of Alby's relatives I'd seen at Enid's wedding. The front pew was empty except for Gran Ryder. Behind us the church was filling up, mostly with families from the Thornfield estate, and pupils and teachers from Herby's. I saw Miss Dowdeswell sitting next to our headmaster, Dr Lang, and just behind them, Dipper Dickson, Tubbo Simms, and several other boys and girls from the Fifth Form. Among them was Helen O'Donnell. I had never seen her dressed in black before, and it seemed to emphasise her beauty and sophistication .

The hushed conversation in the pews stopped abruptly as Alby's coffin appeared at the rear of the chapel carried by four bearers. It was followed down the aisle by Alby's parents and Enid and her husband, with the vicar, the Reverend Ernest Trittiford, bringing up the rear. Mrs Wilson and Enid, both tearful, were holding tightly onto the hands of their spouses. As the four of them sat down with Gran Ryder in the front pew, the bearers placed Alby's coffin on a catafalque behind the altar.

Mr Trittiford mounted the altar steps and turned to face the congregation. First he reminded us of the solemn reason we were gathered there, then launched into a prayer. I heard little of it though, as my mind drifted off into a stream of inconsequential memories - the clink of a tin can being kicked along the pavement by Alby, the high pitched whistle that only he could produce through that gap in his front teeth, his deft fingers dealing a hand of cards. I just hoped the Big Fellah was concentrating on the vicar's words and not noticing the irreverent meanderings going on inside my head.

The sounds of coughing and shuffling feet signaled the end of Mr Trittiford's prayer and his announcement of the first hymn. As the congregation launched into *Make Me A Channel of Your Peace,* I felt a shiver travel up my back. My reading was the next item on the order of service sheet. I reached in my pocket for the folded paper that contained the words from the Gospel of St. John that I had carefully copied from my mother's bible. I read through them for the umpteenth time. As the congregation began the last verse of the hymn, I stood up, feeling self-conscious, and made my way at what I though was a respectful pace to the lectern at the front of the church. I unfolded the sheet with my reading and placed it on top of the large open bible. Waiting for the hymn to end I glanced at the coffin a few

188

feet away and was surprised to feel for the first time since Alby's death a sense of tranquillity. Maybe it had something to do with an acceptance that what now really mattered was not Alby's mortal remains in that wooden box, but something indestructible; call it his spirit, the essence of his being, his immortal soul, the Alby I reckoned was already making his presence felt with the Big Fellah.

These thoughts were drifting through my mind as I heard the congregation singing the last line of the hymn ... *'and in dying that we're born to eternal life.'* As the reverberations of the organ died away, I began reading. 'St John's Gospel, chapter fourteen, verses one to six... Let not your heart be troubled; ye believe in God, believe also in me...' As I read on I was thankful I had learned the piece almost by heart, and by the end felt almost a sense of exhilaration. I wasn't sure if it was the moving quality of the words or simply that I'd read it in just the way I had rehearsed, and without breaking down.

Reverend Trittiford whispered 'Well done, young man,' as I headed back to my seat. I looked to the back of the church where Helen O'Donnell was sitting. As our eyes met momentarily she nodded and put her hands together in front of her face in a gesture of prayer. The future without Alby began to seem just a little less bleak.

The next item on the service sheet was the vicar's address, which contained predictable platitudes about the tragedy of someone dying so young, and God moving in mysterious ways, and how much Alby was loved by everyone. I had an urge to call out, 'Okay, but tell the people what Alby was really all about. Tell them we've lost a genius, a loveable, funny, irreplaceable, independent cuss who was my friend. Tell them the world's lost someone might have changed it for the better.' I doubt though, that Alby would have thanked me for such an outburst, and I expect I would have been mightily embarrassed afterwards.

After another hymn and a prayer, the vicar concluded with an announcement that family and friends were welcome to go on to the Wilsons' house for refreshments after the burial, which was to take place at Ardley Green cemetery. As we filed out to the strains of *The Londonderry Air,* Alby's favourite tune, I decided that if he was watching the proceedings it would probably be with a mixture of incredulity and amusement.

My mother and father and me were given a lift to the cemetery by Alby's Uncle Bill in the Jowett in which I'd been taken to Cornwall.

I don't remember much of the burial ceremony except for the tears, the sticky yellowness of the clay as the coffin was lowered into the grave, and a smattering of the vicar's ritual words: *'The Lord is full of compassion and mercy, slow to anger and of great goodness... We flourish like a flower in the field; when the wind goes over it, it is gone and its place will know it no more... earth to earth, ashes to ashes, dust to dust...'*

As we walked back to the waiting cars, I felt my mother's arm around my shoulder. 'That must have been very hard for you, ' she said.

'I'm glad it's over,' I said.

My father looked as if he was going to say something, then seemed to change his mind and stared straight ahead. Maybe it was wishful thinking, yet I had the feeling he too wanted to comfort me.

We had reached the churchyard gate when Alby's mother and father caught up with us. Cliff Wilson thrust

190

out his hand to my father. 'Thanks for coming, George.'

My father nodded and shook Cliff's hand. 'I thought a lot of Alby. You've lost a fine lad.'

'Will you come back to the house?' asked Cliff.

'Of course we will, won't we George,' said my mother.

My father hesitated, then said, 'Yes, we'll come.'

My mother and Mrs Wilson exchanged glances.

'We'll see you shortly then,' said Mrs Wilson.

'Yes,' said my mother, 'we'll see you shortly.'

CHAPTER TWENTY

Two days after the funeral I went back alone to the Ardley Green cemetery. There, in the quiet of the early evening, I stood beside Alby's grave and opened the letter his mother had passed on to me. It was written on the blank side of a hospital form:

Dear Matt,

I'm writing this on some paper I scrounged from that nurse with the nice little bottom. By the time you read it I shall probably already be making a nuisance of myself with the Big Fellah (always assuming I haven't been sent to the other place). I know I promised to leave you my system for winning at cards etc but at the last minute I had second thoughts. So I tore up the instructions I had written out and decided to write this letter instead. The thing is I always felt a bit uncomfortable taking money off my pals, even though my system was fair and honest, well pretty honest. Also it took a bit of the fun away knowing I could always win, though I admit I got quite a kick out of seeing my system working.

What's more, knowing what a straight up the middle kind of kid you, are you would probably feel even more awkward than I did relieving mates of their pocket money, and you wouldn't even have the satisfaction of knowing you were doing it with a system you had invented. And, most important of

all, why would you need a gambling system,
however foolproof, when you will have your own
personal guardian angel watching over you, ready
to help out whenever your need me.

   Hope all this makes sense. I'm pretty doped
up by the quacks as I write it. Remember, as we
used to say when we both worked for the Secret
Service, this is for your eyes only.

   Have a great life.
   Your (soon to be) guardian angel.
   Alby.

I read the letter again, slowly this time, then tore it
into tiny pieces and scattered them like confetti among the
bunches and sprays of lilies, carnations and
chrysanthemums left by the mourners on Alby's grave. I
looked up into the fading sunlight and gave my newly
installed guardian angel the kind of wink he so often used
to give me when there was a meeting of minds.

END

Lightning Source UK Ltd.
Milton Keynes UK
UKOW03f1052150414

230005UK00001B/19/P